THE ONE
I KNEW THE BEST
OF ALL

HER CHEEKS GREW HOTTER AND HOTTER, SHE READ
FAST AND FURIOUSLY.

(Page 111.)

THE ONE
I KNEW THE BEST
OF ALL

BY

MRS. F. H. BURNETT

AUTHOR OF "LITTLE LORD FAUNTLEROY," "SARA CREWE," ETC., ETC.

WITH ILLUSTRATIONS BY REGINALD BIRCH

LONDON
FREDERICK WARNE AND CO.
BEDFORD STREET, STRAND

First published in Great Britain by
Frederick Warne & Co. in 1893
Facsimile edition © Frederick Warne & Co. Ltd,
London, England, 1974

ISBN 0 7232 1817 X

Printed in Great Britain by William Clowes & Sons Ltd
London, Beccles and Colchester

277:774

PREFACE.

—•—

I should feel a serious delicacy in presenting to the world a sketch so autobiographical if I did not feel myself absolved from any charge of the bad taste of personality, by the fact that I believe I might fairly entitle it "The Story of *any* Child with an Imagination." My impression is that the Small Person differed from a world of others only in as far as she had more or less imagination than other little girls. I have so often wished that I could see the minds of young things with a sight stronger than that of very interested eyes, which can only see from the *outside*. There must be so many thoughts for which child courage and child language have not the exact words. So, remembering that there was one child of whom I could write from the inside point of view, and with certain knowledge, I began to make a little sketch of the one I knew the best of all. In my first intention it was to be only a brief final one for a series of sketches I had made of children I had known in different countries, but when I began it I found so much to record which seemed amusing and illustrative, that the short sketch became a long one. What I have tried to do has been to make a picture, not of a particular child, but of the impressions made upon a child mind as the panorama of Life passed before it, explained only by itself —a picture of the mental impressions of a little unit of whose parallels there are tens of thousands. The Small Person has gone to that far away country where all other Small Persons emigrate as time rolls by—the land to whose unknown countries there wandered some years ago two little fellows I have longed for ever since, as all mothers long for the tender little shadows once realities. Whatsoever the dearness of the maturer creatures the passing years make of them, they speak to us with voices—they smile at us with eyes not quite the same—not quite the same! And to the unknown fairy land where Time leads childhood and leaves it straying, and to the innocent little figures which people it, I think that all of us look backward with tender yearning and sometimes with almost dewy eyes. As I might write

freely of these two small shadows, so I have felt I might
write freely of this Small Person who has so long been a
shadow like themselves.

FRANCES HODGSON BURNETT.

CONTENTS.

xii   *CONTENTS.*

CHAPTER XV.

CHAPTER XVI.

LIST OF ILLUSTRATIONS.

LIST OF ILLUSTRATIONS.

THE ONE I KNEW THE BEST OF ALL.

A MEMORY OF THE MIND OF A CHILD

——◆◆——

CHAPTER I.

THE ONE I KNEW THE BEST OF ALL.

HAD every opportunity for knowing her well, at least. We were born on the same day, we learned to toddle about together, we began our earliest observations of the world we lived in at the same period, we made the same mental remarks on people and things, and reserved to ourselves exactly the same rights of private personal opinion.

I have not the remotest idea of what she looked like. She belonged to an era when photography was not as advanced an art as it is to-day, and no picture of her was ever made. It is a well-authenticated fact that she was auburn-haired and rosy, and I can testify that she was curly, because one of my earliest recollections of her emotions is a memory of the momentarily maddening effect of a sharp, stinging jerk of the comb when the nurse was absent-minded or maladroit.

That she was also a plump little person I am led to believe, in consequence of the well-known joke of a ribald boy cousin and a disrespectful brother, who averred that when she fell she " bounced " like an india-rubber ball. For the rest, I do not remember what the looking-glass reflected back at her, though I must have seen it. It might, consequently, be argued that on such occasions there were so many serious and interesting problems to be attended to that a reflection in the looking-glass was an unimportant detail.

In those early days I did not find her personally interesting—in fact I do not remember regarding her as a personality at all. It was the people about her, the things she saw, the events which made up her small existence, which were absorbing, exciting, and of the most vital and terrible importance sometimes. It was not until I had children of my own, and had watched their small individualities forming themselves, their large imaginations giving proportions and value to things, that I began to remember her as a little Person, and in going back into her past and reflecting on certain details of it and their curious effects upon her, I found interest in her and instruction, and the most serious cause for tender deep reflection on her as a thing touching on that strange, awful problem of a little soul standing in its newness in the great busy, tragic world of life, touched for the first time by everything that passes it, and never touched without some sign of the contact being left upon it.

What I remember most clearly and feel most serious is one
thing above all : it is that I have no memory of any time so
early in her life that she was not a distinct little *individual*.
Of the time when she was not old enough to formulate
opinions quite clearly to herself I have no recollection, and I
can remember distinctly events which happened before she
was three years old. The first incident which appears to me
as being interesting, as an illustration of what a baby mind is
doing, occurred a week or so after the birth of her sister, who
was two years younger than herself. It is so natural, so
almost inevitable, that even the most child-loving among us
should find it difficult to realize constantly that a mite of
three or four, tumbling about, playing with india-rubber
dogs and with difficulty restrained from sucking the paint off
Noah, Shem, Ham, and Japhet, not to mention the animals,
is a *person*, and that this person is ten thousand times more
sensitive to impression than one's self, and that hearing and
seeing one, this person, though he or she may not really
understand, will be likely, in intervals of innocent destruction
of small portable articles, to search diligently in infant
mental space until he or she has found an explanation of
affairs, to be pigeon-holed for future reference. And yet I
can most solemnly declare that such was the earliest habit of
that " One I knew the best of all."

One takes a fat, comfortable little body on one's knee and
begins to tell it a story about " a fairy " or " a doggie " or
" a pussy." And the moment the story begins the questions

begin also. And with my recollection of the intense little
Bogie whom I knew so well and who certainly must have
been a most every-day-looking little personage, giving no outward warning of preternatural alertness and tragic earnest-
ness, my memory leads me to think that indeed it is not a
trifle to be sufficiently upright and intelligent to answer these
questions exactly as one should. This first incident, which
seems to me to denote how early a tiny mind goes through
distinct processes of thought, is a very clear memory to me.

I see a comfortable English bedroom, such as would to-day
seem old-fashioned without being ancient enough to be picturesque. I remember no articles of furniture in the room
but a rather heavy four-posted carved mahogany bed, hung
with crimson damask, ornamented with heavy fringe and big
cords and tassels, a chair by this bedside—I think it was an
arm-chair covered with chintz—and a footstool. This was
called " a buffet," and rhymed with Miss Muffet eating her
curds and whey. In England Miss Muffet sat on " a buffet,"
on the blood-curdling occasion when

> " There came a big spider
> And sat down beside her
> And frightened Miss Muffet away."

This buffet was placed upon the hearth-rug before the fire,
and a very small being was sitting upon it, very conscious,
in a quiet way, of her mamma lying on the crimson-draped
bed, and the lady friend who was sitting in the chair by her,
discussing their respective new babies. But most of all was

the Small Person on the buffet conscious of their own personal new baby who was being taken care of by a nurse just near her.

Perhaps the interest of such recollections is somewhat added to by the fact that one can only recall them by episodes, and that the episodes seem to appear without any future or any past. Not the faintest shadow of the new baby seems to appear upon the camera, up to this moment, of the buffet, and I have no remembrance of any mental process which led to the Small Person's wishing to hold it on her knee. Perhaps it was a sudden inspiration.

But she did wish to hold it, and notified as much, apparently with sufficient clearness, to the nurse.

The shadow of the nurse has no name and no special individuality. She was only a figure known as " The Nurse."

But she impresses me in these days as having been quite definite in her idea that Persons not yet three years old were not to be trusted entirely with the new-born, however excellent their intentions were.

How the Small Person expressed herself in those days I do not know at all. Before three years articulation is not generally perfect, but if hers was not I know she was entirely unaware of her inadequacies. She thought she spoke just as other people did, and I never remember her pronunciation being corrected. I can recall, with perfect distinctness, however, what she *thought* she expressed and what her hearers *seemed* to understand her to say.

It was in effect something like this :

" I want to hold the New Baby on my knee."

" You are too little," said the Nurse.

"No, I am not too little. The New Baby is little, and I am on the buffet, and I will hold her tight if you will put her on my knee."

" She would slip off, I am afraid."

" No, I will hold her tight with both arms, just like you do. Please give her to me." And the Small Person spread her small knees.

I don't know how long the discussion lasted, but the Nurse was a good-natured person, and at last she knelt down upon the hearth-rug by the buffet, holding the white-robed New Baby in her arms and amiably pretended to place it in the short arms and on the tiny knees, while she was really supporting it herself.

"There," she said. "Now she is on your knee." She thought she had made it all right, but she was gravely mistaken.

" But I want to hold her *myself,*" said the Small Person.

" You are holding her," answered the Nurse, cheerfully. "What a big girl to be holding the New Baby just like a grown-up lady."

The Small Person looked at her with serious candour.

" I am *not* holding her," she said. " *You* are holding her."

That the episode ended without the Small Person either

having held the New Baby, or being deceived into fancying
she held it, is as clear a memory to me as if it had occurred
yesterday, and the point of the incident is that after all the
years that have passed I remember with equal distinctness
the thoughts which were in the Small Person's mind as she
looked at the Nurse and summed the matter up, while the
woman imagined she was a baby not capable of thinking
at all.

It has always interested me to recall this because it was so
long ago, and while it has not faded out at all, and I see the
mental attitude as definitely as I see the child and the four-
post bed with its hangings, I recognize that she was too
young to have had in her vocabulary the *words* to put her
thoughts and mental arguments into—and yet they were
there, as thoughts and mental arguments are there to-day
—and after these many years I can write them in adult
words without the slightest difficulty. I should like to have
a picture of her eyes and the expression of her baby face as
she looked at the Nurse and thought these things, but
perhaps her looks were as inarticulate as her speech.

"I am very little," she thought. "I am so little that you
think I do not know that you are pretending that I am holding the New Baby, while really it is you who are holding it.
But I do know. I know it as well as you, though I am so
little and you are so big that you always hold babies. But I
cannot make you understand that, so it is no use talking.
I want the baby, but you think I shall let it fall. I am sure

I shall not.   But you are a grown-up person and I am a little
child, and the big people can always have their own way."

I do not remember any rebellion against an idea of injustice.

YOU ARE A GROWN-UP PERSON AND I AM A LITTLE CHILD.

All that comes back to me in the form of a mental attitude is
a perfect realization of the immense fact that people who
were grown up could do what they chose, and that there was
no appeal against their omnipotence.

It may be that this line of thought was an infant indication of a nature which developed later as one of its chief characteristics, a habit of adjusting itself silently to the inevitable, which was frequently considered to represent indifference, but which merely evolved itself from private conclusions arrived at through a private realization of the utter uselessness of struggle against the Fixed.

The same curiosity as to the method in which the thoughts expressed themselves to the small mind devours me when I recall the remainder of the bedroom episode, or rather an incident of the same morning.

The lady visitor who sat in the chair was a neighbour, and she also was the proprietor of a new baby, though her baby was a few weeks older than the very new one the Nurse held.

She was the young mother of two or three children, and had a pretty, sociable manner towards tiny things. The next thing I see is that the Small Person had been called up to her and stood by the bed in an attitude of modest decorum, being questioned and talked to.

I have no doubt she was asked how she liked the New Baby, but I do not remember that or anything but the serious situation which arose as the result of one of the questions. It was the first social difficulty of the Small Person—the first confronting of the overwhelming problem of how to adjust perfect truth to perfect politeness.

Language seems required to mentally confront this

problem and try to settle it, and the Small Person cannot
have had words, yet it is certain that she confronted and
wrestled with it.

"And what is your New Baby's name to be?" the lady
asked.

"Edith," was the answer.

"That is a pretty name," said the lady. "I have a new
baby, and I have called it Eleanor? Is not that a pretty
name?"

In this manner it was—simple as it may seem—that the
awful problem presented itself. That it seemed awful—
actually almost unbearable—is an illustration of the strange
touching sensitiveness of the new-born butterfly soul just
emerged from its chrysalis—the impressionable sensitiveness
which it seems so tragic that we do not always remember.

For some reason—it would be impossible to tell what—the
Small Person did *not* think Eleanor was a pretty name. On
strictly searching the innermost recesses of her diminutive
mentality she found that she *could* not think it a pretty
name. She tried, as if by muscular effort, and could not.
She thought it was an *ugly* name; that was the anguish of
it. And here was a lady, a nice lady, a friend with whom
her own mamma took tea, a kind lady, who had had the
calamity to have her own newest baby christened by an ugly
name. How could any one be rude and hard-hearted enough
to tell her what she had done—that her new baby would
always have to be called something ugly? She positively

quaked with misery. She stood quite still and looked at the poor nice lady helplessly without speaking. The lady probably thought she was shy, or too little to answer readily or really have any opinion on the subject of names. Mistaken lady: how mistaken, I can remember. The Small Person was wrestling with her first society problem, and trying to decide what she must do with it.

"Don't you think it is a pretty name?" the visitor went on, in a petting, coaxing voice, possibly with a view to encouraging her. "Don't you like it?"

The Small Person looked at her with yearning eyes. She could not say "No" blankly. Even then there lurked in her system the seeds of a feeling which, being founded on a friendly wish to be humane, which is a virtue at the outset, has increased with years, until it has become a weakness which is a vice. She could not say a thing she did not mean, but she could not say brutally the unpleasant thing she did mean. She ended with a pathetic compromise.

"I don't think," she faltered—"I don't think—it is—as pretty—as Edith."

And then the grown-up people laughed gayly at her as if she were an amusing little thing, and she was kissed and cuddled and petted. And nobody suspected she had been thinking anything at all, any more than they imagined that she had been translating their remarks into ancient Greek. I have a vivid imagination as regards children, but if I had been inventing a story of a child, it would not have occurred to me to imagine such a mental episode in such a very tiny person. But the vividness of my recollection of this thing has been a source of interest and amusement to me through so many mature years that I feel it has a certain significance as impressing upon one's mind a usually unrealized fact.

When she was about four years old a strange and serious event happened in the household of the Small Person, an event which might have made a deep and awesome impression on her but for two facts. As it was, a deep impression was made, but its effect was not of awfulness, but of unexplainable mystery. The thing which happened was that the father of the Small Person died. As she belonged to the period of Nurses and the Nursery she did not feel very familiar with him, and did not see him very often. " Papa," in her mind, was represented by a gentleman who had curling brown hair and who laughed and said affectionately funny things. These things gave her the impression of his being a most agreeable relative, but she did not know that the funny things were the jocular remarks with which good-natured maturity generally salutes tender years. He was intimately connected with jokes about cakes kept in the dining-room sideboard, and with amiable witticisms about certain very tiny glasses of sherry in which she and her brothers had drunk his health and her mamma's, standing by the table after dinner, when there were nuts and other fruits adorning it. These tiny glasses, which must really have been liqueur glasses, she thought had been made specially small for the accommodation of persons from the Nursery.

When "papa" became ill the Nursery was evidently kept kindly and wisely in ignorance of his danger. The Small Person's first knowledge of it seemed to reach her through an interesting adventure. She and her brothers and the New Baby, who by this time was quite an old baby, were taken away from home. In a very pretty countrified Public Park, not far away from where she lived, there was a house where people could stay and be made comfortable. The Park still exists, but I think the house has been added to and made into a museum. At that time it appeared to an infant imagination a very splendid and awe-inspiring mansion. It seemed very wonderful indeed to live in a house in the Park where one was only admitted usually under the care of Nurses who took one to walk. The Park seemed to become one's own private garden, the Refreshment Room containing the buns almost part of one's private establishment, and the Policemen, after one's first awe of them was modified, to become almost mortal men.

It was a Policeman who is the chief feature of this period. He must have been an amiable Policeman. I have no doubt he was quite a fatherly Policeman, but the agonies of terror the One I knew the best of all passed through in consequence of his disposition to treat her as a joke, are something never to be forgotten.

I can see now from afar that she was a little person of the

most law-abiding tendencies. I can never remember her feeling the slightest inclination to break a known law of any kind. Her inward desire was to be a good child. Without actually formulating the idea, she had a standard of her own. She did not want to be "naughty," she did not want to be scolded, she was peace-loving and pleasure-loving, two things not compatible with insubordination. When she was "naughty," it was because what seemed to her injustice and outrage roused her to fury. She had occasional furies, but went no further.

When she was told that there were pieces of grass on which she must not walk, and that on the little boards adorning their borders the black letters written said "Trespassers will be prosecuted," she would not for worlds have set her foot upon the green, even though she did not know what "prosecuted" meant. But when she discovered that the Park Policemen who walked up and down in stately solitude were placed by certain awful authorities to "take up" anybody who trespassed, the dread that she might inadvertently trespass some day and be "taken up," caused her blood to turn cold.

What an irate Policeman, rendered furious by an outraged law, represented to her tender mind I cannot quite clearly define, but I am certain that a Policeman seemed an omnipotent power, with whom the boldest would not dream of trifling, and the sole object of whose majestic existence was to bring to swift, unerring justice the juvenile law-breakers who in the madness of their youth drew upon themselves the eagle glance of his wrath, the awful punishment of justice being to be torn shrieking from one's Mamma and incarcerated for life in a gloomy dungeon in the bowels of the earth. This was what "Prison" and being "taken up" meant.

It may be imagined, then, with what reverent awe she regarded this supernatural being from afar, clinging to her Nurse's skirts with positively bated breath when he appeared; how ostentatiously she avoided the grass which must not be trodden upon; how she was filled with mingled terror and gratitude when she discovered that he even descended from his celestial heights to *speak* to Nurses, actually in a jocular manner and with no air of secreting an intention of pouncing upon their charges and "taking them up" in the very wantonness of power.

I do not know through what means she reached the point of being sufficiently intimate with a Policeman to exchange respectful greetings with him and even to indulge in timorous conversation. The process must have been a very gradual one and much assisted by friendly and mild advances from the Policeman himself. I only know it came about, and this I know through a recollection of a certain eventful morning.

It was a beautiful morning, so beautiful that even a Policeman might have been softened by it. The grass which must not be walked upon was freshest green, the beds of flowers upon it were all in bloom. Perhaps the brightness of the sunshine and the friendliness of nature emboldened the Small Person and gave her giant strength.

How she got there I do not know, but she was sitting on one of the Park benches at the edge of the grass, and a Policeman—a real august Policeman—was sitting beside her.

Perhaps her Nurse had put her there for a moment and left her under the friendly official's care. But I do not know. I only know she was there, and so was he, and he was doing nothing alarming. The seat was one of those which have only one piece of wood for a back and she was so little that her short legs stuck out straight before her, confronting her with short socks and plump pink calf and small "ankle-strap" shoes, while her head was not high enough to rest itself against the back, even if it had wished to.

It was this last fact which suggested to her mind the possibility of a catastrophe so harrowing that mere mental anguish forced her to ask questions even from a Minion of the law. She looked at him and opened her lips half a dozen times before she dared to speak, but the words came forth at last :—

" If any one treads on the grass must you take them up ? "

" Yes, I must." There is no doubt but that the innocent fellow thought her and her question a good joke.

" Would you have to take *any one* up if they went on the grass ? "

" Yes," with an air of much official sternness. "*Any* one."

She panted a little and looked at him appealingly. " Would you have to take *me* up if I went on it ? " Possibly she hoped for leniency because he evidently did not object to her Nurse, and she felt that such relationship might have a soften- ing influence.

" Yes," he said, " I should have to take you to prison."

" But," she faltered, " but if I *couldn't help* it—if I didn't go on it on purpose ? "

" You'd have to be taken to prison if you went on it," he said. " You couldn't go on it without knowing it."

She turned and looked at the back of the seat which was too high for her head to reach, and which consequently left no support behind her exceeding smallness.

" But—but," she said, " I am so little I might fall through the back of this seat. If I was to *fall* through on to the grass ·should you take me to prison ? "

What dulness of his kindly nature—I feel sure he was not an unkindly fellow—blinded the Policeman to the terror and consternation which must in some degree have expressed themselves on her tiny face, I do not understand, but he evidently saw nothing of them. I do not remember what his face looked like, only that it did not wear the ferocity which would have accorded with his awful words.

" Yes," he said, " I should have to pick you up and carry you at once to prison."

She must have turned pale ; but that she sat still without further comment, that she did not burst into frantic howls of

despair, causes one to feel that even in those early days she
was governed by some rudimentary sense of dignity and
resignation to fate, for as
she sat there, the short
legs in socks and small
black " ankle - straps "
confronting her, the
marrow was dissolving
in her infant bones.

SHE SAT THERE, THE SHORT LEGS IN SOCKS AND SMALL BLACK "ANKLE-STRAPS"
CONFRONTING HER.

There is doubtless suggestion as to the limits and exaggerations of the tender mind in the fact that this incident was an
awful one to her and caused her to waken in her bed at night

and quake with horror, while the later episode of her hearing that "Poor Papa" had died seemed only to be a thing of mystery of which there was so little explanation that it was not terrible. This was without doubt because, to a very young child's mind, death is an idea too vague to grasp.

There came a day when some one carried her into the bedroom where the crimson-draped four-post bed was, and standing by its side held her in her arms that she might look down at Papa lying quite still upon the pillow. She only thought he looked as if he were asleep, though some one said : "Papa has gone to Heaven," and she was not frightened, and looked down with quiet interest and respect. Seven years later the sight of a child of her own age or near it, lying in his coffin, brought to her young being an awed realization of death, whose anguished intensity has never wholly repeated itself : but being held up in kind arms to look down at "Poor Papa," she only gazed without comprehension and without fear.

CHAPTER II.

THE LITTLE FLOWER-BOOK AND THE BROWN TESTAMENT.

DO not remember the process by which she learned to read or how long a time it took her. There was a time when she sat on a buffet before the Nursery fire—which was guarded by a tall wire fender with a brass top—and with the assistance of an accomplished elder brother a few years her senior, seriously and carefully picked out with a short, fat finger the capital letters adorning the advertisement column of a newspaper.

But from this time my memory makes a leap over all detail until an occasion when she stood by her Grandmamma's knee by this same tall Nursery fender and read out slowly and with dignity the first verse of the second chapter of Matthew in a short, broad, little speckled brown Testament with large print.

"When Jesus—was—born—in—Bethlehem—of Judea," she read, but it is only this first verse I remember.

Either just before or just after the accomplishing of this feat she heard that she was three years old. Possibly this fact was mentioned as notable in connection with the reading, but to her it was a fact notable principally because it was the first time she remembered hearing that she was any age at all and that birthdays were a feature of human existence.

But though the culminating point of the learning to read

SHE STOOD BY HER GRANDMAMMA'S KNEE . . . . AND READ OUT SLOWLY THE FIRST VERSE
OF THE SECOND CHAPTER OF MATTHEW.

was the brown Testament, the process of acquiring the accomplishment must have had much to do with the " Little Flower-book."

In a life founded and formed upon books, one naturally looks back with affection to the first book one possessed. The one known as the "Little Flower-book" was the first in the existence of the One I knew the best of all.

No other book ever had such fascinations, none ever contained such marvellous suggestions of beauty and story and adventure. And yet it was only a little book out of which one learned one's alphabet.

But it was so beautiful. One could sit on a buffet and pore over the pages of it for hours and thrill with wonder and delight over the little picture which illustrated the fact that A stood for Apple-blossom, C for Carnation, and R for Rose. What would I not give to see those pictures now. But I could not see them now as the Small Person saw them then. I only wish I could. Such lovely pictures! So like real flowers! As one looked at each one of them there grew before one's eyes the whole garden that surrounded it—the very astral body of the beauty of it.

It was rather like the Brown Testament in form. It was short and broad, and its type was large and clear. The short page was divided in two; the upper half was filled with an oblong black background, on which there was a flower, and the lower half with four lines of rhyme beginning with the letter which was the one that "stood for" the flower. The black background was an inspiration, it made the flower so beautiful. I do not remember any of the rhymes, though I have a vague impression that they usually treated of some moral attribute which the flower was supposed to figuratively represent. In the days when the Small Person was a child, morals were never lost sight of; no well-regulated person ever mentioned the Poppy, in writing for youth, without calling it "flaunting" or "gaudy;" the Violet, without laying stress on its "modesty;" the Rose, without calling attention to its "sweetness," and daring indeed would have been the individual who would have referred to the Bee without calling him "busy." Somehow one had the feeling that the Poppy was deliberately scarlet from impudence, that the Violet stayed up all night, as it were, to be modest, that the Rose had invented her own sweetness, and that the Bee would rather perish than be an "idle butterfly" and not spend every moment "improving each shining hour." But we stood it very well. Nobody repined, but I think one rather had a feeling of having been born an innately vicious little person who needed labouring with constantly that one might be made merely endurable.

It never for an instant occurred to the Small Person to resent the moral attributes of the flowers. She was quite resigned to them, though my impression is that she dwelt on them less fondly than on the fact that the rose and her alphabetical companions were such visions of beauty against their oblong background of black.

The appearing of the Flower-book on the horizon was an event in itself. Somehow the Small Person had become devoured by a desire to possess a book and know how to read

it. She was the fortunate owner of a delightful and ideal
Grandmamma—not a modern grandmamma, but one who
might be called a comparatively "early English" grandmamma. She was stately but benevolent; she had silver-
white hair, wore a cap with a full white net border, and
carried in her pocket an antique silver snuff-box, not used as
a snuff-box, but as a receptacle for what was known in that
locality as "sweeties," one of which being bestowed with
ceremony was regarded as a reward for all nursery virtues
and a panacea for all earthly ills. She was bounteous and
sympathetic, and desires might hopefully be confided to her.
Perhaps this very. early craving for literature amused her,
perhaps it puzzled her a little. I remember that a
suggestion was tentatively made by her that perhaps a doll
would finally be found preferable to a book, but it was
strenuously declared by the Small Person that a book, and
only a book, would satisfy her impassioned cravings. A
curious feature of the matter is that, though dolls at a later
period were the joy and the greater part of the existence of
the Small Person, during her very early years I have
absolutely no recollection of a feeling for any doll, or indeed
a memory of any dolls existing for her.

So she was taken herself to buy the book. It was a
beautiful and solemn pilgrimage. Reason suggests that it
was not a long one, in consideration for her tiny and brief
legs, but to her it seemed to be a journey of great length—
principally past wastes of suburban brick-fields, which for

some reason seemed romantic and interesting to her, and it ended in a tiny shop on a sort of country road. I do not see the inside of the shop, only the outside, which had one small window, with toys and sweet things in glass jars. Perhaps the Small Person was left outside to survey these glories. This would seem not improbable, as there remains no memory of the interior. But there the Flower-book was bought (I wonder if it really cost more than sixpence) ; from there it was carried home under her arm, I feel sure. Where it went to, or how it disappeared, I do not know. For an æon it seemed to her to be the greater part of her life, and then it melted away, perhaps being absorbed in the Brown Testament and the more dramatic interest of Herod and the Innocents. From her introduction to Herod dated her first acquaintance with the "villain" in the drama and romance, and her opinion of his conduct was, I am convinced, founded on something much larger than mere personal feeling.

CHAPTER III.

THE BACK GARDEN OF EDEN.

DO not know with any exactness where it was situated. To-day I believe it is a place swept out of existence. In those days I imagine it was a comfortable, countrified house, with a big garden round it, and fields and trees before and behind it; but if I were to describe it and its resources and surroundings as they appeared to me in the enchanted days when I lived there, I should describe a sort of fairyland.

If one could only make a picture of the places of the world as these Small Persons see them, with their wondrous proportions and beauties—the great heights and depths and masses, the garden-walks which seem like stately avenues, the rose-bushes which are jungles of bloom, the trees adventurous brothers climb up and whose topmost branches seem to lift them to the sky. There was such a tree at the bottom of the garden at Seedly. To the Small Person the garden seemed a mile long. There was a Front Garden and a Back Garden, and it was the Back Garden she liked best and which appeared to her large enough for all one's world. It was all her world during the years she spent there. The

Front Garden had a little lawn with flower-beds on it and a gravel walk surrounding it and leading to the Back Garden. The interesting feature of this domain was a wide flower-bed which curved round it and represented to the Small Person a stately jungle. It was filled with flowering shrubs and trees which bloomed, and one could walk beside them and look through the tangle of their branches and stems and imagine the things which might live among them and be concealed in their shadow. There were rose-bushes and lilac-bushes and rhododendrons, and there were laburnums and snowballs. Elephants and tigers might have lurked there, and there might have been fairies or gypsies, though I do not think her mind formulated distinctly anything more than an interesting suggestion of possibilities.

But the Back Garden was full of beautiful wonders. Was it always Spring or Summer there in that enchanted Garden which, out of a whole world, has remained throughout a lifetime the Garden of Eden? Was the sun *always* shining? Later and more material experience of the English climate leads me to imagine that it was not *always* flooded and warmed with sunshine, and filled with the scent of roses and mignonette and new-mown hay and apple-blossoms and strawberries all together, and that when one laid down on the grass on one's back one could not always see that high, high world of deep sweet blue with fleecy islets and mountains of snow drifting slowly by or seeming to be quite still —that world to which one seemed somehow to belong even more than to the earth, and which drew one upward with such visions of running over the white soft hills and springing, from little island to little island, across the depths of blue which seemed a sea.   But it was always so on the days the One I knew the best of all remembers the garden.   This is no doubt because, on the wet days and the windy ones, the cold days and the ugly ones, she was kept in the warm nursery and did not see the altered scene at all.

In the days in which she played out of doors there were roses in bloom, and a score of wonderful annuals, and bushes with gooseberries and red and white and black currants, and raspberries and strawberries, and there was a mysterious and endless seeming alley of Sweetbriar, which smelt delicious when one touched the leaves, and which sometimes had a marvellous development in the shape of red berries upon it.   How is it that the warm, scented alley of Sweetbriar seems to lead her to an acquaintance, an intimate and friendly acquaintance, with the Rimmers's pigs, and somehow through them to the first Crime of her infancy.

The Rimmers were some country working-people whose white-washed cottage was near the Back Garden.   Rimmer himself was a market-gardener, and in his professional capacity had some connection with the Back Garden itself, and also with the gardener.   The cottage was very quaint and rural, and its garden, wherein cabbages and currant-bushes and lettuces, etc., grew luxuriantly, was very long and narrow, and one of its fascinating features was the pig-sty.

A pig-sty does not seem fascinating to mature years, but to Six-years-old, looking through an opening in a garden hedge and making the acquaintance of a little girl pig-owner on the other side, one who knows all about pigs and their peculiarities, it becomes an interesting object.

Not having known the pig in his domestic circles, as it were, and then to be introduced to him in his own home, surrounded by Mrs. Pig and a family of little Pink Pigs, squealing and hustling each other, and being rude over their dinner in the trough, is a situation full of suggestion.

The sty is really like a little house. What is he thinking of as he lies with his head half-way out of the door, blinking in the sun, and seeming to converse with his family in grunts? What do the grunts mean? Do the little Pink Pigs understand them? Does Mrs. Pig really reply when she seems to? Do they really like potato and apple parings, and all sorts of things jumbled together with buttermilk and poured into the trough?

The little girl whose father owns the pigs is very gifted. She seems to know everything about the family in the sty. One may well cherish an acquaintance with a person of such knowledge and experience.

One is allowed to talk to this little girl. Her name is Emma Rimmer. Her father and mother are decent people, and she is a well-behaved little girl. There is a little girl whose mother keeps the toll-gate on the road, and it is not

permitted that one should converse with her. She is said to
be "a rude little girl," and is tabooed.

But with Emma Rimmer it is different. She wears a print
frock and clogs, and speaks in the Lancashire dialect, but
there seems to be no serious objection to occasional conversation with her. At some time the Small Person must
have been taken into the narrow garden, because of a remembrance of luxuries there revealed. A yard or so from the
door of the cottage there was a small wooden shed, with a
slanting roof protecting a sort of table or counter, with
toothsome delicacies spread upon it for sale.

They were refreshments of the sort which the working
classes patronize during their Sunday walks into the country.
Most of them are purchasable for one penny, or one halfpenny, in coin of the realm. Pieces of cardboard in the
cottage window announce :

> "Pop. A penny a bottle.
> Ginger beer
> Sold here.
> Also Nettle beer."

On the stall there are "Real Eccles Cakes. One penny
each." "Parkins. A halfpenny." There are glass bottles
with "Raspberry Drops" in them, and "Bull's Eyes," and
"Humbugs"—beautiful striped sticky things which taste
strongly of peppermint. If one is capitalist enough to
possess a halfpenny, one can spend half an hour in trying to
decide what luxury to invest it in.

There was in those days in the air a rumour—for which Emma Rimmer was responsible—a sort of legend repeated with bated breath and not regarded with entire confidence— of a female Monte Cristo of tender years, who once had spent a whole sixpence at a time. But no one saw her. She was never traced and could not have belonged to the neighbourhood. Indeed there was an impression in the Small Person's mind that she was somehow connected with some one who worked in factories—perhaps was a little factory girl herself. No well-regulated little girl, with a nurse's eye upon her, would have been permitted to indulge in such reckless, even vulgar, extravagance.

Through the nearness of these temptations Crime came. The Serpent entered the Back Garden of Eden. The Serpent was innocent little Emma Rimmer.

There was a day on which the Small Person was playing with Emma Rimmer. Perhaps the air was sharp and hunger-creating, perhaps she had not eaten all her bowl of bread-and-milk at her Nursery breakfast that morning. Somehow she was not in the Back Garden, but in the road outside the big gates which opened into the carriage-way. Why she was without her Nurse is not explained. She seemed to be jumping about and running in a circle with Emma Rimmer, and she became suddenly conscious of a gnawing sense of vacancy under the belt of her pinafore. "I am so hungry," she said; "I am so hungry." Emma looked at her and then continued to jump up and down.

Something unusual must have been in the situation,
because there seemed to be none of the usual methods to fall
back upon in the way of going in search of bread-and-
butter.

"I wish I had a halfpenny," she continued. "If I had a
halfpenny I would get you to go to your cottage and get me
a halfpenny parkin." A parkin is a spicy thing made of
molasses and oatmeal and flavoured with ginger. It can only
be found in Lancashire and Yorkshire.

Emma stopped jumping and looked sharply reflective.
Familiarity with commerce had rendered her daring.

"Why doesna' tha' go an' get a parkin on trust?" she
said. "My mother'd trust thee for a ha'p'ny."

"Ah!" gasped the Small Person.

The boldness of the suggestion overwhelmed her. She had
never dreamed of the possibility of such a thing.

"Aye, she would," said Emma. "Tha' could just get thy
parkin an' pay next toime tha' had a ha'p'ny. A moit o'
people does that way. I'll go an' ax Mother fur thee
now."

The scheme seemed so gigantic, so far from respectable, so
fraught with peril. Suppose that one got a parkin "on
trust," and *never* got a halfpenny, and one's family were consequently involved in eternal dishonour and disaster.

"Mamma would be angry," she said; "she would not let
me do it."

"Tha' needn't say nowt about it," said Emma.

This was not actual duplicity, I am convinced. Her stolid rusticity retained its red cheeks like rosy apples, and she hopped about like a cheerful sparrow.

"IF I HAD A HALFPENNY I WOULD GET YOU TO GO TO YOUR COTTAGE AND GET ME A HALFPENNY PARKIN."

It was doubtless this serene and matter-of-fact unconsciousness of any serious aspect of the matter which had its effect upon the Small Person. There is no knowing how long the discussion lasted, or in what manner she was finally per-

suaded by prosaic, practical argument that to make an
investment " on trust " was an every-day commercial affair.
The end of the matter was that stress of the moment pre-
vailed and Emma went for the parkin.

But the way of the infant transgressor is hard.   The sense
of proportion is as exaggerated in regard to mental as to
physical objects.   As lilac and rhododendron bushes form
jungles, and trees reach the sky, so a nursery law defied
assumes the stature of a crime, and surrounds itself with
horror.   I do not think there is a defalcator, an absconding
bank president, a criminal of any degree, who is beset by
such a monster of remorse as beset the Small Person when
her guilt was so far an accomplished fact that the brown and
sticky cake was in her hand.

The incident is nothing, but its effect, in its illustration of
the dimensions facts assume to the contemplative mind of
tender years, has its interest.   She could not eat the " parkin."   Her soul revolted against it after the first bite.   She
could not return it to Mrs. Rimmer with a semi-circular piece
taken out of its roundness, and the marks of small, sharp teeth
on the edge.   In a situation so fraught with agony and so
clouded with infamy she could confide in no one.   I have never
murdered any one and had the body of my victim to conceal
from the public eye, but I know how a murderer suffering
from this inconvenience feels.   The brown, sticky cake with
the semi-circular bite taken out of it, was as awful and as
difficult to manage.   To dispose of it involved creeping about

on tiptoe, with beating heart and reeling brain. It involved looking stealthily for places where evidences of crime might be concealed. Why the Small Person hit on a specially candid shelf in a cupboard in an undisguised sideboard in the dining-room, as a good place, it would be difficult to say. I comfort myself by saying that this indicated that she was naturally unfitted for crime and underhanded ways, and was not the least clever in stealth.

How she separated from her partner in iniquity I do not remember. My chief memory is of the awful days and nights which followed. How many were there? She thought a thousand—it is probable there were two or three.

She was an infant Eugene Aram, and the body of her victim was mouldering in the very house with her. Her anguish, however, did not arise from a fear of punishment. Her Mamma was not severe, her Nurses were not allowed to slap her. It was a mental affair altogether. She felt that she had disgraced her family. She had brought ignominy and dishonour upon her dearest relatives. She was very fond of her relatives, and her conception of their moral and mental altitude was high. Her Mamma was a lady, and her little daughter had gone and bought a halfpenny parkin " on trust." She would have felt it not the least undue thing if a thunder-bolt had struck her dead in the Back Garden. It was no longer the Back Garden of Eden. A degraded criminal defiled it with her presence.

And the Body was mouldering in the sideboard, on the second shelf in the little cupboard.

I think she would have faded away and perished with the parkin, as witch-stricken victims perish with the waxen figure which melts—but there came relief.

She had two brothers older than herself, and so to be revered, as representing experience and the powerful mind of masculinity. (Being an English little girl she knew the vast superiority of the Male.) The younger of the two was a combative little fellow with curly hair, a belted-in roundabout, a broad white collar, and two broad white front teeth. As she was only a girl, he despised her in a fraternal British way, but as she was his sister he had a kind of affection for her, which expressed itself in occasional acts of friendly patronage. He was perhaps seven or eight years old.

In some moment of severest stress of anguish she confessed herself to him. It is so long ago that I cannot describe the manner or the occasion. I can only remember the magnificence of his conduct. He must have been a good-natured little fellow, and he certainly had a lordly sense of the family dignity, even as represented or misrepresented by a girl.

That he berated her roundly it is not unlikely, but his points of view concerning the crime were not as disproportionately exalted as her own. His masculine vigour would not permit her to be utterly crushed, or the family honour lost. He was a man and a Capitalist, as well as a Man and a Brother. He had a penny of his own, he had also a noble and Napoleonic nature. He went to the cottage of Mrs. Rimmer (to his greater maturity was accorded the freedom of leaving the garden unaccompanied by a nurse) *and paid for the parkin.* So the blot was erased from the escutcheon, so the criminal, though still feeling herself stained with crime, breathed again.

She had already be-gun to have a sort of literary imagination, and it must in some way have been already fed with some stories of heroic and noble little boys whose conduct was to be emulated and ad-mired. I argue this from the fact that she mentally and reverently

IN SOME MOMENT OF SEVEREST STRESS OF ANGUISH SHE CONFESSED HERSELF TO HIM.

compared him to a boy in a book. What book I cannot say, and I am not sure that she could have said herself, but at that time he figured in her imagination as a creature too noble to be anything but a creation of literature—the kind of boy who would refuse to steal apples, and invariably gave his plum-cake to beggars or hungry dogs.

But there was a feature of the melting away of this episode

which was always a mystery to her. Her Mamma knew all,
so did her Grandmamma, so did the Nurses, and yet she was
not treated as an outcast. Nobody scolded her, nobody
reviled her, nobody seemed to be afraid to leave her with the
Baby, for fear she might destroy it in some mad outburst of
her evil instincts. This seemed inexplicable. If she had
been branded on the brow, and henceforth kept under the
custody of a strong escort of policemen, she would not have
been surprised. And yet she was allowed to eat her breakfast bowl of bread-and-milk at the Nursery table with innocent children, and to play in the Back Garden as if her
presence would not blight the gooseberries, and the red currants
would not shrivel beneath her evil eye.

My opinion is that, hearing the story from the Capitalist in
the roundabout, her Mamma and her Grandmamma were
privately immensely amused, and felt it more discreet to preserve a dignified silence. But that she was not swept from
the earth as she deserved, did not cause her to regard her
crime as less. She only felt the wonderfulness of mercy as
embodied in one's Grandmamma and one's Mamma.

CHAPTER IV.

LITERATURE AND THE DOLL.

WHETHER as impression - creating and mind-moulding influences, Literature or the Doll came first into her life it would be most difficult to decide. But remembering the rôle the Doll played, and wherein its fascination lay, I see that its way must have been paved for it in some rudimentary manner by Literature, though their clearly remembered existences seem to have begun at one and the same time. Before the advent of literary influence I remember no Doll, and curiously enough, there is, before the advent of the Doll, a memory of something like stories—imperfect, unsatisfactory, filling her with vague, restless craving for greater completeness of form, but still creating images for her, and setting her small mind at work.

It is not in the least likely she did not own dolls before she owned books, but it is certain that until literature assisted imagination and gave them character, they seemed only things stuffed with sawdust and made no special impression.

It is also certain that she cannot have been told stories as a rule. I should say that she did not hear them even as the

exception.   I am sure of this because I so well recollect her
desperate efforts to wring detail of any sort from her
Nurses.

The "Slaughter of the Innocents" seems to me to have
been the first story impression in her life.   A little illustrated
scripture history afforded a picture of Jewish mothers rushing madly down broad stone stairways clasping babies to their
breasts, of others huddling under the shadow of high walls
clutching their little ones, and of fierce armed men slashing
with swords.

This was the work of Herod the King.   And "In Rama
was there a voice heard, lamentation and weeping, and great
mourning.   Rachel weeping for her children, and would not
be comforted, because they were not."

This was the first story, and it was a tragedy — only
made endurable by that story of the Star in the East which
led the way to the Manger where the little Child lay sleeping
with a light about his head—the little Child before whom the
wise men bent, worshipping and offering gifts of frankincense
and myrrh.   She wondered greatly what frankincense and
myrrh were, but the wise men were beautiful to her, and
she could see quite clearly the high deep dome of blue which
vaulted the still plain where the Shepherds watched their
flocks at night, when the Angel of the Lord came to them
and glory shone round about and they were "sore afraid,"
until the angel said unto them, "Fear not, for behold, I
bring you good tidings of great joy."

This part of the story was strange and majestic and lovely, and almost consoled her for Herod the King.

The Nurse who was the unconscious means of suggesting to her the first romance of her life, must have been a dull person. Even at this distance I find myself looking back at her vague, stupid personality with a sense of impatience.

How could a person learn a couple of verses of a song suggesting a story, and not only neglect to learn more, but neglect to inquire about the story itself.

And oh, the helpless torture of hearing those odd verses and standing by that phlegmatic person's knee with one's yearning eyes fixed on her incomprehensible countenance, finding one's self unable to extort from her by any cross-examination the details !

Even the stray verses had such wonderful suggestion in them. They opened up such vistas. At that time the Small Person faithfully believed the song to be called " Sweet Alice Benbolt "—Miss Alice Benbolt being, as she supposed, the name of the young lady described in the lines. She was a very sensitive young lady, it appeared, from the description given in the first verse :

> " Ah, don't you remember Sweet Alice Benbolt,
> Sweet Alice with hair so brown ;
> How she wept with delight when you gave her a smile,
> And trembled with fear at your frown ? "

It did not then occur to the Small Person that Miss Benbolt must have been trying in the domestic circle ; she was so moved by the tender image of a brown-haired girl who was called "Sweet Alice" and set to plaintive music. Somehow there was something touching in the way she was spoken of—as if people had loved her and were sorry about her for some reason—the boys had gone to the school-house "under the hill," connected with which there seemed to be such pathetic memories, though the Small Person could not comprehend why they were pathetic. But there was a pathos in one verse which broke her heart when she understood it, which she scarcely did at first :

> "In the little churchyard in the valley Benbolt,
> In a corner obscure and alone,
> They have fitted a slab of the granite so grey,
> And sweet Alice lies under the stone "

"Why does she lie there ? " she asked, with both hands on the Nurse's knee. "Why does Sweet Alice lie under the stone ? "

"Because she died," said the Nurse, without emotional compunctions, "and was buried there."

The Small Person clung rather helplessly to her apron.

"Sweet Alice," she said, "Sweet Alice with hair so brown ? "

(Why was the brown hair pathetic as well as the name ? I don't know. But it was.)

"Why did she die ? " she asked. "What did she die for ? "

"I don't know," said the Nurse.

"But—but—tell me some more," the Small Person gasped. "Sing some more."

"I don't know any more."

"But where did the boys go?"

"I don't know."

"What did the schoolmaster do?"

"The song doesn't tell."

"Why was he grim?"

"It doesn't tell that either."

"Did Sweet Alice go to school to him?"

"I dare say."

"Was he sorry when she died?"

"It does not say."

"Are there no more verses?"

"I can't remember any more."

Questioning was of no use. She did not know any more and she did not care. One might implore and try to suggest, but she was not an imaginative character, and so the Small Person was left to gaze at her with hungry eyes and a sense of despair before this stolid being, who *might* have known the rest and would not. She probably made the woman's life a burden to her by imploring her to sing again and again the stray verses, and I have no doubt that at each repetition she invented new questions.

"Sweet Alice Benbolt," she used to say to herself. "Sweet Alice with hair so brown." And the words always called up in her mind a picture which is as clear to-day as it was then.

It is a queer little picture, but it seemed very touching at that time. She saw a hillside covered with soft green. It was not a high hill and its slope was gentle. Why the "school-house under the hill" was placed on the top of it, would be difficult to explain. But there it was, and it seemed to look down on and watch benignly over something in a corner at the foot of it. The something was a slab of the granite so grey lying among the soft greenness of the grass.

"And Sweet Alice lay under the stone."

She was not a shadow—Sweet Alice. She is something far more than a shadow even now, in a mind through which thousands of shadows have passed. She was a tender thing —and she had brown hair—and somehow people loved her —and she died.

It was not until Literature in the form of story, romance, tragedy, and adventure had quickened her imagination that the figure of the Doll loomed up in the character of an absorbing interest, but once having appeared it never retired from the scene until advancing years forced the curtain to fall upon the exciting scenes of which it was always the heroine.

That was the truth of the matter—it was not a Doll, but a Heroine.

And some imagination was required to make it one. The Doll of that day was not the dimpled star-eyed creature of to-day, who can stand on her own firm little feet, whose plump legs and arms can be placed in any position, whose attitudes may be made to express emotions in accordance with the Delsarte system, and who has parted lips and pearly teeth, and indulges in features. Not at all.

The natural advantages of a doll of that period confined themselves to size, hair which was sewn on a little black skull-cap—if it was not plastered on with mucilage—and eyes which could be jerked open if one pulled a wire which stuck out of her side. The most expensive and magnificent doll you could have was merely a big wax one, whose hair could be combed and whose eyes would open and shut. Otherwise they were all the same. Only the face and neck were of wax, and features were not studied by the manufacturers. All the faces were exactly the same shape, or rather the same shapelessness. Expression and outline would have been considered wanton waste of material. To-day dolls have cheeks and noses and lips and brows, they look smiling or pensive, childlike or sophisticated. At that time no doll was guilty of looking anything at all. In the middle of her smooth round face was a blunt excrescence which was called a nose, beneath it was a line of red paint which was meant for a mouth, on each side of it was a tight-looking black or blue glass eye as totally devoid of expression and as far removed from any resemblance to a real eye as the combined talents of ages of doll manufacturers could make it. It had no pupil and no meaning, it stared, it glared, and was only a little more awful when one pulled the

wax lid over it than it was when it was fixed and open.   Two
arches of brown paint above it were its eyebrows, and all
this beauty was surmounted with the small black cap on the
summit of which was stretched a row of dangling curls of
black or brown.   Its body was stuffed with sawdust, which
had a tragic tendency to burst forth and run out through
any hole in the white calico which was its skin.   The arms
and legs were like sawdust-stuffed sausages, its arms were
covered with pink or blue or yellow or green kid, there being
no prejudice caused by the fact that arms were not usually
of any of these shades; its legs dangled painfully and
presented no haughty contours, and its toes invariably
turned in.

How an imagination, of the most fervid, could transform
this thing into a creature resembling anything human one
cannot explain.   But nature is very good—sometimes—to
little children.   One day, in a squalid London street, I drove
by a dirty mite sitting upon a step, cuddling warmly a little
bundle of hay tied round the middle with a string.   It was
her baby.   It probably was lily fair and had eyes as blue as
heaven, and cooed and kissed her again—but grown-up people
could not see.

When I recall the adventures through which the Dolls of
the Small Person passed, the tragedies of emotion, the
scenes of battle, murder, and sudden death, I do not wonder
that at times the sawdust burst forth from their calico cuticle
in streams, and the Nursery floor was deluged with it.   Was

it a thing to cause surprise that they wore out and only lasted from one birthday to another ? Their span of life was short, but they could not complain that existence had not been full for them. The Doll who, on November 24th, begins a chequered career by mounting an untamed and untamable, fiercely prancing and snorting steed, which, while it strikes sparks from the earth it spurns with its disdainful hoofs, wears to the outward gaze the aspect of the mere arm of a Nursery Sofa covered with green baize—the Doll who begins life by mounting this steed, and so conquering its spirit that it responds to her touch and leaps the most appalling hedges and abysses, and leaves the lightning itself behind in its career; and having done this on the 24th, is executed in black velvet on the 25th as Mary Queen of Scots, besides being imprisoned in the Tower of London as some one else, and threatened with the rack and the stake because she will not " recant " and become a Roman Catholic—a Doll with a career like this cannot be dull, though she may at periods be exhausted. While the two little sisters of the Small Person arranged their doll's house prettily and had tea-parties out of miniature cups and saucers, and visited each other's corners of the Nursery, in *her* corner the Small Person entertained herself with wildly-thrilling histories, which she related to herself in an undertone, while she acted them with the assistance of her Doll.

She was all the characters but the heroine—the Doll was that. She was the hero, the villain, the banditti, the pirates,

the executioner, the weeping maids of honour, the touchingly
benevolent old gentleman, the courtiers, the explorers, the
king.

She always spoke in a whisper or an undertone, unless she
was quite alone, because she was shy of being heard. This
was probably an instinct at first, but it was a feeling intensi-
fied early by finding out that her habit of "talking to
herself," as others called it, was considered a joke. The
servants used to listen to her behind doors and giggle when
they caught her, her brothers regarded her as a ridiculous
little object. They were cricket-playing boys, who possibly
wondered in private if she was slightly cracked, but would
have soundly thumped and belaboured any other boy who
had dared to suggest the same thing.

The time came when she heard it said that she was
"romantic." It was the most crushing thing she had ever
experienced. She was quite sure that she was not romantic.
She could not bear the ignominy of the suggestion. She did
not know *what* she was, but she was *sure* she was not
romantic. So she was very cautious in the matter of keeping
to her own corner of the Nursery and putting an immediate
stop to her performance the instant she observed a silence, as
if any one was listening. But her most delightful life con-
centrated itself in those dramatized stories through which
she "talked to herself."

At the end of the entrance hall of the house in which she
lived was a tall stand for a candelabra. It was of worked

iron and its standard was ornamented with certain decorative supports to the upper part.

What were the emotions of the Small Person's Mamma, who was the gentlest and kindest of her sex, on coming upon her offspring one day, on descending the staircase, to find her apparently furious with insensate rage, muttering to herself as she brutally lashed with one of her brother's toy whips, a cheerfully hideous black

SHE WAS LASHING THAT POOR BLACK DOLL AND TALKING TO HERSELF LIKE A LITTLE FURY.

gutta-percha doll who was tied to the candelabra stand and appeared to be enjoying the situation.

"My dear, my dear!" exclaimed the alarmed little lady, "what *are* you doing?"

The Small Person gave a little jump and dropped at her side the stalwart right arm which had been wielding the whip. She looked as if she would have turned very red, if it had been possible for her to become redder than her exertions had made her.

"I—I was only playing," she faltered, sheepishly.

"Playing!" echoed her Mamma. "What *were* you playing?"

The Small Person hung her head and answered, with downcast countenance, greatly abashed,—

"I was—only just—*pretending* something," she said.

"It really quite distressed me," her Mamma said, in discussing the matter afterward with a friend. "I don't think she is really a *cruel* child. I always thought her rather kind-hearted, but she was lashing that poor black doll and talking to herself like a little fury. She looked quite wicked. She said she was 'pretending' something. You know that is her way of playing. She does not play as Edith and Edwina do. She 'pretends' her doll is somebody out of a story and she is somebody else. She is very romantic. It made me rather nervous the other day when she dressed a baby-doll in white and put it into a box and covered it with flowers and buried it in the front garden. She was so absorbed in it, and she hasn't dug it up. She goes and strews flowers over the grave. I should like to know what she was 'pretending' when she was beating the black doll."

Not until the Small Person had outgrown all dolls, and her mother reminded her of this incident, did that innocent lady know that the black doll's name was Topsy, but that on this occasion it had been transformed into poor Uncle Tom, and that the little fury with the flying hair was the wicked Legree.

She had been reading " Uncle Tom's Cabin." What an era it was in her existence! The cheerful black doll was procured immediately and called Topsy; her " best doll," which fortunately had brown hair in its wig, was Eva, and was kept actively employed slowly fading away and dying, while she talked about the New Jerusalem, with a hectic flush on her cheeks. She converted Topsy, and totally changed her gutta-percha nature, though it was impossible to alter her gutta-percha grin. She conversed with Uncle Tom (then the Small Person was Uncle Tom), she cut off " her long golden-brown curls" (not literally; that was only " pretended ": the wig had not ringlets enough on it), and presented them to the weeping slaves. (Then the Small Person was all the weeping slaves at once.) It is true that her blunt-nosed wax countenance remained perfectly unmoved throughout all this emotion, and it must be confessed that at times the Small Person felt a lack in her, but an ability to " pretend " ardently was her consolation and support.

It surely must be true that all children possess this right

of entry into the fairyland where *anything* can be " pretended." I feel quite sure they do, and that if one could follow them in the " pretendings," one would make many discoveries about them. One day in the Cascine in Florence a party of little girls passed me. They were led by a handsome child of eleven or twelve who, with her head in the air, was speaking rapidly in French.

" Moi," she said to the others as she went by, and she made a fine gesture with her hand, " Moi, je suis la Reine ; vous— vous êtes ma suite ! "

It set one to thinking. Nature has the caprice sometimes, we know, to endow a human thing at birth with gifts and powers which make it through life a leader—" *la reine*" or " le roi," of whom afterwards others are always more or less " la suite." But one wondered if such gifts and powers in themselves had not a less conscious and imperious air than this young pretender wore.

The green-covered sofa in the Nursery was an adventurous piece of furniture. To the casual observer it wore a plain old-fashioned, respectable exterior. It was hard and uninviting and had an arm at each end under which was fitted a species of short, stiff green bolster or sausage. But these arms were capable of things of which the cold unimaginative world did not dream. I wonder if the sofa itself dreamed of them, and if it found them an interesting variety of its regular Nursery life. These arms were capable of transforming themselves at a moment's notice in the most superb equine form. They were " coal-black steeds " or " snow-white palfreys," or " untamed mustangs ; " they " curvetted," they " caracoled," they pranced, their " proud hoofs spurned the earth." They were always doing things like these, while the Doll " sprang lightly to her saddle," or sat " erect as a dart." They were always untamable, but the Doll in her character of heroine could always tame them and remain smiling and fearless while they " dashed across the boundless plain " or clawed the heavens with their forefeet. No equestrian feat ever disturbed the calm hauteur of the Doll. She issued triumphant from every deadly peril.

It was Sir Walter Scott who transformed the sofa-arms to " coal-black steeds," G. P. R. James and Harrison Ainsworth who made them " snow-white palfreys," and Captain Mayne Reid whose spell changed them to " untamed mustangs " and the Nursery into a boundless prairie across which troops of Indian warriors pursued the Doll upon her steed, in paint and feathers, and with war-whoops and yells, having as their object in view the capture of her wig.

What a beautiful, beautiful story the " War Trail " was—with its white horse of the prairie which would not be caught. How one thrilled and palpitated in the reading of it. It opened the gateway to the world of the prairie, where the herds of wild horse swept the plain, where buffaloes stampeded, and Indian chieftains, magnificent and ferocious and always covered with wampum (whatever wampum might be), pursued heroes and heroines alike.

And the delight of Ainsworth's "Tower of London." That beloved book with the queer illustrations. The pictures of Og, Gog, and Magog, and Xit the Dwarf, Mauger the Headsman, the Crafty Renard, the Princess Elizabeth with Courtenay kneeling at her feet, and poor embittered Queen Mary looking on.

What a place it was for a Small Person to wander through in shuddering imaginings, through the dark, dank subterranean passages, where the rats scurried, and where poor mad Alexia roamed, persecuted by her jailer! One passed by dungeons where noble prisoners pined through years of dying life, one mounted to towers where queens had waited to be beheaded, one was led with chilling blood through the dark Traitors' gate. But one reached sometime or other the huge kitchen and servitors' hall, where there was such endless riotous merriment, where so much "sack" and "Canary" was drunk, where there were great rounds of roast beef, and "venison pasties," and roast capons, and even peacocks, and where they ate "manchets" of bread and "quaffed" their flagons of nut-brown ale, and addressed each other as "Sirrah," and "Varlet," and "Knave," in their elephantine joking.

Poor little Lady Jane Grey! Poor, handsome, misguided Guildford Dudley! Poor anguished, terrified, deluded Northumberland!

What tragic, historical adventures the Doll passed through in these days; how she was crowned, discrowned, sentenced, and beheaded, and what horror the Nursery felt of wretched, unloved, heretic-burning Bloody Mary! And through these tragedies the Nursery Sofa almost invariably accompanied her as palfrey, scaffold, dungeon, or barge from which she " stepped to proudly, sadly, pass the Traitors' Gate."

And if the Nursery Sofa was an endeared and interesting object, how ungrateful it would be to ignore the charms of the Green Arm Chair in the Sitting-Room, the Sitting-Room Cupboard, and the Sitting-Room Table. It would seem simply graceless and irreverent to write the names of these delightful objects, as if they were mere common nouns, without a title to capital letters. They were benevolent friends who lent their aid in the carrying out of all sorts of fascinating episodes, who could be confided in, as it were, and trusted never to laugh when things were going on, however dramatic they might be.

The sitting-room was only a small one, but somehow it had an air of seclusion. It was not the custom to play in it, but when nobody was there and the nursery was specially active it had powerful attractions. One could go in there with the Doll and talk to one's self when the door was shut, with perfect freedom from fear of listeners. And there was the substantial sober-looking Arm Chair—as sober and respectable as the Nursery Sofa, and covered with the same green stuff, and it could be transformed into a " bark " of any description from a pinnace to a gondola, a canoe, or a raft set afloat by the survivors of a sinking ship to drift

for weeks upon "the trackless ocean" without water or
food.

Little incidents of this description were continually taking
place in the career of the Doll. She was accustomed to
them. Not a hair of her wig turned at the agreeable
prospect of being barely rescued from a burning ship, of
being pursued all over the Indian Ocean or the Pacific by
a "rakish-looking craft" flying the black flag and known to
be manned by a crew of bloodthirsty pirates, whose amusement of making captives walk the plank was alternated by
the scuttling of ships. It was the head pirate's habit to
attire himself almost wholly in cutlasses and pistols, and to
greet the appearance of any prepossessing female captive
with the blood-curdling announcement, "She shall be
mine!" But the Doll did not mind that in the least, and it
only made it thrilling for the hero who had rescued her from
the burning ship. It was also the opinion of the Small
Person that no properly constituted pirate chief could possibly
omit greeting a female captive in this manner—it rather
took, in fact, the form of a piratical custom. The sitting-
room floor on these occasions represented mid-ocean—the
Pacific, the Indian, or the Mediterranean Sea, their waters
being so infested with sharks and monsters of the deep (in
order that the hero might plunge in and rescue the Doll,
whose habit it was to fall overboard) that it was a miracle
that it was possible at all to steer the Green Arm Chair.

But how nobly and with what nautical skill it was steered

by the hero! The crew was necessarily confined to the Doll and this unconquerable being—because the Green Arm Chair was not big.

But notwithstanding his heroic conduct, the cold judgment of maturer years has led me to believe that this young man's mind must either have been enfeebled by the hardships through which he had passed, or that the ardour of his passion for the Doll had caused his intellect to totter on its throne. I am led to this conviction by my distinct recollection of the fact that on the occasion of some of their most perilous voyages, when the Doll had been rescued at the peril of his noble life, the sole article which he rescued with her, as being of practical value upon a raft, was a musical instrument. An indifferent observer who had seen this instrument in the hand of the Small Person might have coarsely supposed it to be a tin whistle—of an order calculated to make itself specially unpleasant—but to the hero of the raft and to the Doll it was known as " a lute." Why, with his practical knowledge of navigation, the hero should have felt that a rescued young lady on a raft, without food or water, might be sustained in moments of collapse from want of nutrition by performances upon the " lute " only persons of deep feeling and sentiment could explain. But the lute was there and the hero played on it, in intervals of being pursued by pirates or perishing from starvation with appropriately self-sacrificing sentiments. For myself I have since thought that possibly the tendency the Doll developed for falling into the depths of the ocean arose from an unworthy desire to distract the attention of her companion from his musical rhapsodies. He was, of course, obliged to lay his instrument aside while he leaped overboard and rescued her from the sharks, and she may have preferred that he should be thus engaged. Were my nature more hardened than years have as yet made it, I might even say that at times she perhaps thought that the sharks might make short work of his lute—or himself—and there *may* have been moments when she scarcely cared which. It *must* be irritating to be played to on a lute, when one is perishing slowly from inanition.

But ah! the voyages in the Green Arm Chair, the seas it sailed, the shores it touched, the enchanted islands it was cast upon! The Small Person has never seen them since. They were of the fair world she used to see as she lay upon her back on the grass in the Back Garden of Eden, and looked up into the sky where the white islands floated in the blue. One could long for a no more perfect thing than that; after the long years of wanderings on mere earth, one might find them again, somewhere—somewhere. Who knows where?

How surprised the governess would have been, how amused the mamma, how derisive in their ribald way the brothers, if they had known that the Sitting-Room Cupboard was a temple in Central America—that the strange pigmy remnants of the Aztec royal race were kept there and worshipped as gods, and that bold explorers, hearing of their mysterious existence, went in search of them in face of all danger and difficulty and with craft and daring discovered and took them away. All these details were in a penny pamphlet which had been sold at the hall of the exhibition where the two Aztec dwarfs had been on view, the object of the scientific explorer having apparently been to make a good thing of them by exhibiting them at a shilling a head, children half price.

The Small Person had not been taken to see them ; in fact, it is possible that the exhibition had not belonged to her time. But at some time, some member of her family must have been of their audience, for there was the pamphlet, with extraordinary woodcuts of the explorers, woodcuts of the Aztecs with their dwarfed bodies and strange receding profiles, and woodcuts of the temple where they had been worshipped as the last remnant of a once magnificent, now practically extinct, royal race.

The woodcuts were very queer, and the Temple was apparently a ruin, whose massive broken and fallen columns made it all the more a place to dwell upon in wild, imaginative dreams. Restored, in the Sitting-Room Cupboard, it was a majestic pile. Mystic ceremonials were held there, splendid rites were solemnized. The Doll took part in them, the Small Person officiated. Both of them explored, both discovered the Aztec. To do so it was necessary to kneel on the floor with one's head inside the cupboard while the scenes were enacted, but this in no wise detracted from the splendour

of their effect and the intensity of their interest. Nothing
could. The Sitting-Room Table must have been adorned
with a cover much too large for it, or else in those days table-
covers were intended to be large. This one hung down so far
over the table that when one sat on the floor underneath it
with the Doll, it became a wigwam. The Doll was a squaw
and the Small Person a chief. They smoked the calumet and
ate maize, and told each other stories of the war-trail and the
happy hunting-grounds. They wore moccasins, and feathers,
and wampum, and brought up pappooses, and were very
happy. Their natures were mild. They never scalped any-
one, though the tomahawk was as much a domestic utensil as
the fire-irons might have been if they had had an Indian
flavour. That it was dark under the enshrouding table-cloth
made the wigwam all the more realistic. A wigwam with bay
windows and a chandelier would not have been according to
Mayne Reid and Fenimore Cooper. And it was so shut out
from the world there, one could declaim—in undertones—
with such freedom. It seemed as if surely *outside* the wall of
the table-cloth there was no world at all—no real world—it
was all under the Sitting-Room Table—inside the wigwam.
Since then I have often wondered what the grown-up people
thought, who, coming into the room, saw the table-cloth drawn
down, and heard a little voice whispering, whispering, whispering, beneath its shadow. Sometimes the Small Person
did not know when they came or went, she was so deeply
absorbed—so far away.

Ah, the world went very well then. It was a wonderful world—so full of story and adventure and romance. One did not need trunks and railroads; one could go to Central America, to Central Africa—to Central Anywhere—on the arm of the Nursery Sofa—on the wings of the Green Arm Chair —under the cover of the Sitting-Room Table.

There is a story of the English painter Watts which I always remember as a beautiful and subtle thing, though it is only a brief anecdote.

He painted a picture of Covent Garden Market, which was a marvel of picturesque art and meaning. One of his many visitors—a lady—looked at it long and rather doubtfully.

"Well, Mr. Watts," she said, "this is all very beautiful, of course, but *I* know Covent Garden Market and I must confess *I* have never seen it look like this."

"No?" replied Watts. And then, looking at her thoughtfully, "Don't you wish you could!"

It was so pertinent to many points of view.

As one looks back across the thousand years of one's life, to the time when one saw all things like this—recognizing how far beyond the power of maturer years it is to see them so again, one says with half a smile, and more than half a sigh:

"Ah, does not one wish one could!"

CHAPTER V.

ISLINGTON SQUARE.

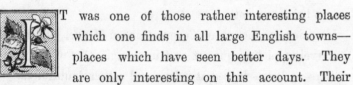T was one of those rather interesting places
which one finds in all large English towns—
places which have seen better days. They
are only interesting on this account. Their
early picturesqueness has usually been destroyed by the fact
that a railroad has forced its way into their neighbourhood, or factories, and their accompanying cottages for operatives have sprung up around them. Both these things had
happened to Islington Square, and only the fact that it was
an enclosed space shut in by a large and quite imposing iron
gateway, aided it to retain its atmosphere of faded gentility.
Such places are often full of story, though they have no air
of romance about them. The people who live in them have
themselves usually seen better days. They are oftenest
widowed ladies with small incomes, and *un*widowed gentlemen
with large families—people who not having been used to
cramped quarters, are glad to find houses of good size at a
reduced rent.

Some of the houses in the Square were quite stately in

proportion, and in their better days must have been fine
enough places. But that halcyon period was far in the past.
Islington Hall—the most imposing structure—was a "Select
Seminary for young ladies and gentlemen;" its companion
house stood empty and deserted, as also did several others
of the largest ones, probably because the widowed ladies and
unwidowed gentlemen could not afford the corps of servants
which would have been necessary to keep them in order.

In the centre of the Square was a Lamp Post. I write it
with capital letters because it was not an ordinary lamp post.
It was a very big one, and had a solid base of stone which all
the children thought had been put there for a seat. Four or five
little girls could sit on it, and four or five little girls usually
did when the day was fine.

Ah! the things which were talked over under the Lamp
Post, the secrets that were whispered, and the wrongs that
were discussed! In the winter, when the gas was lighted at
four o'clock, there could be no more delightfully secluded spot
for friendly conversation than the stone base of the lamp which
cast its yellow light from above.

Was it worldly pride and haughtiness of spirit which gave
rise, in the little girls who lived in the Square, to a sense of
exclusiveness which caused them to resent an outside little
girl's entering the iron gates and sitting "on the Lamp
Post?" They always spoke of it as "sitting on the Lamp
Post."

"Who is that sitting on the Lamp Post?" would be said,

disapprovingly. "She is not a Square girl, we don't want Street children sitting on our Lamp Post."

"Street children" were those who lived in the streets surrounding the Square, and as they were in most cases not desirable young persons, they were not considered eligible for the society of "Square children" and the Lamp Post.

When the Small Person was introduced to her first copy of the stories of Hans Christian Andersen, she found a sketch which had a special charm for her. It was called "The Old Street Lamp," and it seemed to be the story of the Lamp in the middle of the Square. It seemed to explain a feeling of affection she had always had for it—a feeling that it was not quite an inanimate object. She had played about it and sat on the stone, and had seen it lighted so often that she loved it, though she had never said so even to herself. She slept in a front room with her mamma, in the very four-post bed which had been a feature in the first remembered episode of her life. Her house exactly faced the Lamp Post, and at night its light shone in at her bedroom window and made a bright patch on the wall. She used to lie and think about things by the gleam of it, and somehow she never felt quite alone. She would have missed it very much if it had not watched over her. At that time street lamps were not lighted in an instant by a magic wand. A lamplighter came with a ladder over his shoulder. He placed the ladder against the post and ran up it with what seemed astonishing rapidity, and after lighting the gas ran down again, shouldered his ladder, and walked off.

How the Small Person adored the novel called " The Lamp-lighter ; " how familiar the friendly lamp seemed to her, and how she loved old Uncle True ! Was there ever such a lov-able old man—were there ever sufferings that moved one to such tears as Gerty's ?

The Street children, as I have said, were not considered desirable companions for the " Square children." The Square was at that time a sort of oasis in the midst of small thoroughfares and back streets, where factory operatives lived and where the broadest Lancashire dialect throve. It was difficult enough to preserve to children any purity of enuncia-tion in a neighbourhood of broadest vowels, and as manner of speech is in England a mark of breeding, association with the Street children was not encouraged.

But the Small Person adored Street children. She adored above all things the dialect they spoke, and the queer things they said. To stray into a forbidden back street and lure a dirty little factory child into conversation was a delight. To stand at the iron gateway at twelve o'clock and see the factory people streaming past, and hear the young women in tied-back aprons and with shawls over their heads, shouting friendly or derisive chaff to the young men and boys in corduroys, was as good as a play—in fact a great deal better than most plays.

She learned to speak the dialect as well as any of them, though it was a furtively indulged in accomplishment. She had two or three clever little girl friends who were fluent in it, and who used it with a rich sense of humour. They used

SITTING ON THE LAMP POST.

to tell each other stories in it, and carry on animated conversations without losing a shade of its flavour. They said

"Wilt tha" and "Wheer art goin'," and "Sithee lass," and
"Eh! tha young besom, tha!" with an easy familiarity
which they did not display in the matter of geography.
There was a very dirty little boy whose family lived rent free,
as care-takers in one of the deserted big houses, and this
dirty little boy was a fount of joy. He had a disreputable
old grandfather who was perennially drunk, and to draw forth
from Tommy, in broadest Lancashire dialect, a cheerfully
realistic description of "Granfeyther" in his cups, was an
entertainment not to be despised. Granfeyther's weakness
was regarded by Tommy in the light of an amiable solecism,
and his philosophical good spirits over the matter presented
a point of view picturesquely novel to the Small Person and
her friends. "Eh! tha should heer my Granfeyther sweer
when he's drunk," Tommy would remark with an air of
triumph suggesting a decent family pride. "Tha shouldst
just heer him. *Tha* never heerd nothin' loike it—*tha*
didn't!" with an evident sense of the limited opportunities
of good society.

It was the habit of the Small Person to sit upon the floor
before one of the drawing-room windows each evening, and
learn her lessons for the next day; and on one of these
occasions she saw a creature who somehow puzzled and interested her intensely, though she could not have explained why.

It was part of an unwritten law that people who did not
occupy houses in the Square should not come into it, unless
they had business. This possibly arose from the fact that it

was not a thoroughfare, and there was really no reason why outsiders should pass the iron gates.

When they did they were always regarded with curiosity until one knew what they wanted. This limitation, in fact, gave the gravelled enclosure surrounded by factories and small streets something of the social atmosphere of a tiny, rather gossipy, country town. Each household knew the other, and had a knowledge of its affairs only limited by the characteristics and curiosities of the members.

So, on this particular evening, when the Small Person, hearing voices, looked up from her geography to see a group of stranger children gathered about the Lamp Post, she put her elbows on the window-sill and her cheeks on her hands, and looked out at them with interest.

They were evidently not only " Street children," but they were " Back Street children," a race more exciting to regard as objects, because their customs and language were, as it were, exotic. " Back Street children " *always* spoke the dialect, and the adult members of their families almost invariably worked in the factories—often, indeed, the children worked there themselves. In that locality the atmosphere of the *foyer* was frequently of a lively nature, generally the heads of the families evinced a marked partiality for beer, and spent their leisure moments in consuming " pots " of it at " th' Public." This not uncommonly resulted in argument of a spirited nature, entered into, quite probably, in the street, carried on incoherently, but with vigour, on the doorsteps, and settled—with the fire-irons or portable domestic articles—in the home circle. Frequently these differences of opinion were terminated with the assistance of one or more policemen ; and while the discussions were being carried on the street was always filled with a mob of delighted and eagerly sympathetic neighbours. Feeling always ran high among the ladies, who usually stood and regarded the scene with arms akimbo.

"A noice chap he is! " it would be said sometimes. " He broke th' beer jug ower 'er 'ed two week sins,' an' now he's give her a graidely black eye. He out to be put i' th' Lockups."

Or—

" No wonder he gi'es her a hidin'. Her spends all his wage at th' Black Pig i' th' beer. She was drunk o' Thursday, an' drunk o' Friday, an' now she's gettin' ready fur Saturday neet."

" A row in Islington Court! " or, " A row in Back Sydney Street. Man beating his wife with a shovel! " was a cry which thrilled the bolder juvenile spirits of the Square with awsome delight. There were even fair little persons who hovered shudderingly about the big gates, or even passed them, in the shocked hope of seeing a policeman march by with somebody in custody.

And the strangers gathered about the Lamp Post were of this world.

They were half a dozen girls or more. Most of them

factory girls in print frocks, covered by the big coarse linen apron, which was tied all the way down the back to confine their skirts, and keep them from being caught by the machinery. They had no bonnets on, and they wore clogs on their feet. They were all the ordinary type of small factory girl—all but one. Why did the Small Person find her eyes fixed upon that one, and following her movements? She was bigger than the others, and seemed more mature, though a child could not have explained why. She was dressed exactly as they were—print frock, tied-back apron, clogs, and bare head, and she held a coarse blue worsted stocking, which she was knitting as she talked. It did not occur to the Small Person that she was beautiful. At that age beauty meant to her something with pink cheeks and sparkling blue or black eyes, and sweetly curled hair, and a charming frock. Not a strange-looking, colourless factory girl, knitting a worsted stocking and wearing wooden clogs. Certainly not.

And yet at that girl she stared, quite forgetting her geography.

The other girls were the ordinary rough lot, talking loudly, bouncing about and pushing each other. But this one was not playing at all. She stood or moved about a little, with a rather measured movement, knitting all the time her blue worsted stocking. She was about sixteen, but of rather massive and somehow majestic mould. The Small Person would have said she was "big and slow," if she had been trying to describe her. She had a clear, colourless face, deep, large grey eyes, slender, but strong, straight black brows, and a rather square chin with a cleft in it. Her hair was dark and had a slight large wave, it was thick and drawn into a heavy knot on the nape of her neck, which was fine and full like a pillar, and held her head in a peculiar stately way.

The Small Person, as she watched her, came to the decision that there was "something the matter with her."

"What is it?" she said, mentally, with a puzzled and impressed feeling. "She's not a bit like the others. She does not look like a Back Street girl at all, though she has got clogs on. Somehow she's different."

That was it. She was different. That was why one could not return to one's geography while one could watch her.

Her companions seemed to appeal to her as if she were a sort of power and influence. She seemed to control them when they made too much noise, though she went on knitting her stocking. The windows were closed, and it was not possible to hear what was said, but occasionally loudly spoken dialect words or phrases reached the Small Person. The group did not stay long, and when it went the one who was "different" led it, and the looker-on watched her out of sight, and pondered a moment or so with her nose flattened against the glass, before she went back to her geography.

One evening the next week, at about the same time, the same group appeared again. The Small Person was again on the floor with her lessons on her knee, the factory girls were still laughing and boisterous, and the one who was different was again knitting.

The Small Person shuffled all her books off her knee and let them drop in a heap on the carpet. She put her elbows on the window-sill again, and gave herself up to absorbed contemplation.

That the other girls shouted and giggled was not interesting, but it was interesting to see how, in the midst of the giggles and shouts, the big one seemed a stately, self-contained creature who belonged to another world. Somehow she seemed strangely to suggest a story which one could not read, and of which one could not guess at the plot.

When she grew older and knew more of people and lives and characters, the Small Person guessed that she *was* a story—this strong, pale creature with the stately head and square-cleft chin. She was that saddest story of all, which is beauty and fineness and power—a splendid human thing born into a world to which she does not belong by any kinship, and in which she must stand alone and struggle in silence and suffer. This was what was the matter with her, this was why a ten-year-old child, bearing in her own breast a thermometer of the emotions, dropped her lesson-books to look at her, and gazed restless and dissatisfied because she could not explain to herself why this one was " different."

This evening the group did not leave the place as they had done before.

Some girl, turning round toward the entrance, caught sight of an approaching figure, and hastily, and evidently in some consternation, elbowed a companion. Then they all looked.

A man was coming toward them—an ill-looking brute in corduroys, with his hands in his pockets and a moleskin cap pulled over his brows. He slouched forward as if he were in a bad temper.

"Here's thy feyther!" cried one of the girls. And she said it to the one who was knitting. She looked at the advancing man and went on knitting as if nothing was occurring. The Small Person would have given all her lesson-books—particularly the arithmetic—to know what he had come for. She knew the kind of man. He usually drank a great deal of beer and danced on his wife in his clogs when depressed or irritated. Sometimes he " punsed " her to death if he had been greatly annoyed, and females were rather afraid of him.

But the girl with the deep eyes and straight black brows evidently was not. She was also evidently used to him. He went up to her and addressed her with paternal blasphemy. He seemed to be ordering her to go home. He growled, and bullied her, and threatened her with his fist.

The Small Person had a horrible fear that he would knock her down and kick her, as was the custom of his class. She felt she could not bear it, and had a wild idea of dashing out somewhere for a policeman.

But the girl *was* different. She looked him straight in the brutal face and went on knitting.   Then she turned and walked slowly out of the Square.   He walked behind her, threatening her at intervals with his fist and his lifted clog.

"Dom tha brazent impidence!" the Small Person heard him say once.

BUT THE GIRL WALKED CALMLY BEFORE HIM.

But the girl walked calmly before him without a word or a hurried movement.   She went on knitting the stocking until she turned the corner and disappeared for the last time from the Small Person's sympathetic gaze.   She also disappeared from her life, for the little girl never saw her again.

But she thought of her often and pondered her over, and felt her a power and a mystery. Not until she had given some contemplative thought to various antique marbles, and had wondered " what was the matter " with the Venus of Milo, did it dawn upon her mind that in this girl in the clogs and apron she had seen and been overpowered by Beauty such as goddesses were worshipped for, and strength such as should belong to one who ruled. She always wanted to know what happened afterward, but there was no end to the story that she ever saw. So it was that some years later she wrote a beginning, a middle, and an end herself. She made the factory operative a Pit Girl, and she called her Joan Lowrie.

There was such food for the imagination in thus living surrounded by the lives of streets full of people who belonged to another world than one's own—a world whose customs, manners, and language were wholly foreign in one sense— where even children got up before daylight and went to their work in the big, whirring, oil-smelling factories—where there was a possibility of being caught by the machinery and carried afterward to the Infirmary, followed by a staring, pitying crowd—a broken, bleeding heap of human suffering lying decently covered on a stretcher. Such accidents were such horrors that to a child mind they seemed always impending, though their occurrence was not frequent. But the mere possibility of them made one regard these people—who lived among the ghastly wheels—with awe.

On the same floor with the Nursery was a room where the governess slept, presiding over an extra bed which contained two little girls.   There was a period when for some reason the Small Person was one of them.   The window of this room, which was at the back, looked down upon the back of the row of cottages in which operatives lived.   When one glanced downward it was easy to see into their tiny kitchens and watch them prepare their breakfasts, and eat them too, if one were curious.

Imagine, then, the interest of waking very early one dark winter's morning and seeing a light reflected on the ceiling of the Nursery bedroom from somewhere far below.

The Small Person did this once, and after watching a little, discovered that not only the light and the window itself were reflected, but two figures which seemed to pass before it or stand near it.

It was too exciting to watch alone, so she spoke to her sister, who slept at her side.

" Edith ! " she whispered, cautiously, for fear of disturbing the governess, " Edith, do wake up.   I want to show you something."   The prospect of being shown something in what appeared to be the middle of the night, was a thing to break any slumbers.

Edith turned and rubbed her eyes.

" What is it ? " she asked, sleepily.

" It's a man and a woman," whispered the Small Person, half under the bed-clothes, " Back Street people in their kitchen. You can see them on our ceiling. *This* ceiling; just look."

Edith looked. Back Street people always awakened curiosity.

" So we can," she said, with a carefully smothered giggle. " There the woman is now ! "

" She's got something in her hand," said the Small Person. " It looks like a loaf."

" It's a piece of *something*," whispered Edith.

" It must be a loaf," said the Small Person. " They're factory people, and the man's wife must be getting his breakfast before he goes to work. I wonder what poor people have for breakfast."

" There's the man ! " exclaimed Edith, with so much animation that the governess turned in her sleep.

" Hush," warned the Small Person ; " she'll wake up and scold us for making a noise."

" The man is washing his face on the dresser," said Edith, in more discreet tones. " We can see what they do when they are near the window. I can see him rubbing and wiggling his head."

" So can I," said the Small Person. " Isn't it fun ? I hope the roller-towel is near the window."

The little whispers, cautious as they were, penetrated the drowsy ears of the governess. She half awakened.

" Children," she said, " what are you whispering about ? Don't be so naughty. Go to sleep ! "

All very well for a sleepy governess, but for two little persons awake at four o'clock, and with front seats at a Back Street panorama on their own bedroom ceiling, ridiculously out of the question.

Ah, the charm of it! The sense of mystery and unusualness. It seemed the middle of the night. In all the bedrooms through the house, every one was asleep—the servants, the brothers, mamma, the very Doll had had her wire pulled and her wax eyelids drawn down. Being awake had the charms of nursery guilt in it. It was naughty to be awake, and it was breaking rules to talk. But how could one go to sleep with the rest when the Back Street woman was awake and getting her husband's breakfast? One's own ceiling reflected it and seemed to include one in the family circle.

"If they had a fight," whispered Edith, "we could see it."

There was no end of speculation to be indulged in. What each figure was really doing when it was near enough to the window to be reflected, what it did when it moved away out of the range of reflection, and what it was possible they said to each other, were all things to be excitedly guessed at, and to endanger the repose of the governess.

"Edith, you are a naughty girl," she said. "Frances, I shall speak to your mamma. Edith would not be whispering if you were not with her. Go to sleep this instant!"

As if going to sleep was a thing done by touching an electric button.

How they longed to creep out of bed, and peep through

the window down into the Back Street people's kitchen itself. But that was out of the question. Neither of them would have dared such an insubordination—the first morning, at least.

But there were other such mornings. It became a habit to waken at that delightful and uncanny hour, just for the pleasure of lying awake and watching the Woman and the Man. That was what they called them. They never knew what their names were, or anything about them, except what was reflected during that early breakfast hour upon the ceiling.

But the Small Person was privately attached to them, and continually tried to imagine what they said. She had a fancy that they were a decent couple, who were rather fond of each other, and it was a great comfort to her that they never had a fight.

CHAPTER VI.

A CONFIDENCE BETRAYED.

S the age of seven years an age of special development, or an age which attracts incidents interesting, and having an effect on life, and
the formation of character? As I look back
I remember so many things which seemed to happen to
the Small Person when she was seven years old. She was
seven or thereabouts when she discovered the Secrétaire;
seven when she began to learn the Lancashire dialect, and
study Back Street people; seven when she first saw Death,
with solemn, asking eyes and awe in her soul; seven when
she wrote her first inarticulate story, which was a poem; and
seven when she was first brought face to face with the
enormity of a betrayed confidence.

Thank God, she did not quite realize what had happened
to her, and that her innocence gave her every reason for hope
disappointed but the true one, that she had been trifled with
and deceived; and thank Heaven, also, that the point involved was not one cruel enough to leave a deep wound. In
fact, though it was quite a serious matter with her, she was

more mystified and disappointed than hurt, and for some
time did not realize that she had been the subject of one of
maturity's jokes.

She had a passion for babies. She seldom pretended that
the Doll was a baby, but a baby—a new baby—was an object
of rapturous delight to her. She liked them very new indeed
—quite red, and with little lace caps on, and disproportionately long clothes. She never found them so delightful as
when they wore long clothes. When their frocks were made
short, and one could see their little red or white shoes kick-
ing, the bloom seemed to have gone off—they were no longer
real babies. But when the nurse seemed to be obliged to
move them carefully lest they should fall into minute frag-
ments, when their mouths always opened when one kissed
them, and when they were fragrant of warm flannel, warm
milk, and violet powder, they were the loves of her yearning
little soul.

There were one or two ladies in the Square who were given
to new babies, and when one of their number honoured the
neighbourhood, the Small Person was always one of the first
to hear of it.

" Did you know," it would be said by some little individual,
" that Mrs. Roberts has got a new baby ? "

Then joy would reign unconfined in the Small Person's
breast. The Doll would be given a day's holiday. Her sawdust interior somehow seemed such an evident thing. She
would be left in her chair to stare, while her proprietor

hovered about the Roberts house, and walked with friends past it, looking up at the windows, and discussing with bated breath, as to whether the new baby was a girl or a boy. I think she had a predilection for girls, feeling somehow that they tended to long clothes for the greater length of time.

Then some day, having had her hair neatly curled, and a clean tucker put in her frock, she would repair to the Roberts establishment, stand on her tiptoes, cautiously ring the bell, and await with beating heart the arrival of the housemaid, to whom she would say, with the utmost politeness of which she was capable :

" If you please, Mamma's compliments, and how is Mrs. Roberts—And if she is as well as can be expected, do you think I might see the new baby ? "

And then, if fortune favoured her, which it usually did, she would be led up the staircase and into a shaded room, which seemed pervaded by a solemn but beautiful stillness which made her feel as if she wanted to be a good little girl always. And Mrs. Roberts, who perhaps was not really a specially handsome person at all, but who looked somehow rather angelic, would hold out her hand and say gently :

" How do you do, my dear ? Have you come to see the new baby ? "

And she would answer in a voice full of respectful emotion :

" Yes, if you please, Mrs. Roberts. Mamma said I might

ask you if I could see it—if you are as well as can be expected—and I may only stay a few minutes for fear I should bother you ? "

" Give my regards to your Mamma, love, and say I'm getting on very nicely, and the baby is a little boy. Nurse will let you look at him."

Oh, to stand beside that lovely bundle and look down at it reverently, as it lay upon the nurse's knee ! Reverence and adoration mingled with awe were the pervading emotions in her small mind. Reverence for Mrs. Roberts and awe of a stately mystery in the shaded room, which made it feel rather like a church, reverence for the nurse who knew all about new babies, reverence for the new baby, whose newness made him seem such a potentate, and adoration — pure, deep *adoration* of him as a Baby.

As years before she had known thoughts which even her mind could not have known words to frame, so in these days I well remember that she felt emotions her child-thoughts could give no shape to, and which were still feelings which deeply moved her. She was only a child, who had been kept a child by those who loved her, who had been treated always as a child, and who was not in any sense old beyond her brief years. And yet my memory brings clearly to me that by the atmosphere of these shaded rooms she was moved and awed as she was later by the atmosphere of other rooms shaded by blinds drawn down—and by the mystery of another stillness—a more awful stillness—a colder one, in which people

always stood weeping as they looked down at Something
which was not a life beginning, but a life's end.

She was too much a little girl to know then that before the
shaded stillness of both chambers the human nature of her
stood hushed and reverent, confronting Mystery, and the
Unanswered Question before which ages have stood hushed
just as she did though she was only seven years old. She
knew no less than all the world.

If the nurse was a kind one she was allowed to look at
the baby's feet, and perhaps to kiss them. Such tiny feet,
so pink and tender, and so given to curling up and
squirming!

"Aren't they weenty," she would say, clasping her hands,
"and isn't he beautiful! Oh, I *wish* he was mine!"

The unbiassed opinion of maturer years leads me to a
tardy conviction that the new babies were *not* beautiful, that
they were painfully creased and grievously red, and had
frequently a weird air of eld combined with annoyance; that
they had no hair and no noses, and no individuality except
to the Mrs. Roberts of the occasion, who saw in them the
gifts and graces of the gods. (This being the lovely boon of
Nature, whom all women of earth may kneel and bless that
she, in some strange, gentle moment, has given them this
thing.)

But it was the serious belief of the Small Person that a
new baby was always Beautiful, and she could not possibly
have understood the creature who insinuated, even with the

most cautious and diplomatic mildness, that it was not. No, that would have been striking at the foundations of the universe.

And there were Nurses who let her *hold* the new baby. She was so careful and so full of tender respect that I think any one might have trusted her—even with twins. When she sat on a low chair and held the white draperied, faintly moving bundle which was a new-born human thing, she was an unformed, yearning Mother-creature, her little breast as warm with brooding instincts as a small bird-mother covering her first nest. She did not know this—she was too young —but it was true.

She was walking slowly round the Square one lovely summer evening, just after tea (Nursery breakfasts were at eight, dinners at one, tea at six), and she had as her companion the little girl who was known as her "Best Friend." One had a best Doll, a best frock, and a best friend. Her best friend was a very sensitive, shy little girl with lovely brown velvet eyes. Her name was Annie, and their souls were one.

As they walked they saw at length a respectable elderly person dressed in black, and carrying something in her arms. It was something white and with long drapery depending from it. She was walking slowly up and down as if taking the air.

"There is a lady with a baby," exclaimed the Small Person. "And it looks like a new one."

"It is a new one," said Annie. "She isn't a Square lady, I wonder who she is."

It was not easy to tell. She was no one they knew, and yet there she was walking quietly up and down, giving a promenade to a new baby.

There was no doubt about the matter, she must be approached. They eyed her wistfully askance, and then looked at each other with the same thought in their eyes.

"Would she think we were rude if we spoke to her?" suggested the Small Person, almost in a whisper.

"Oh, we don't know her," said the little Best Friend. "She might think it very rude."

"Do you think she would?" said the Small Person. "She looks kind," examining her with anxiety.

"Let us walk past her," said the Best Friend. So they walked past her slowly, respectfully regarding the new baby. The elderly lady who carried it did not look vicious, in fact, she looked amiable, and after they had walked past her twice she began to smile at them. This was so encouraging that they slackened their pace and the Best Friend gave the companion of her soul a little "nudge" with her elbow.

"Let's ask her," she said. "You do it."

"No, you."

"I daren't."

"I daren't either."

"Oh, *do*. It's a perfectly new one."

"Oh, *you* do it. See, how nice she looks."

They were quite near her, and just at that juncture she smiled again so encouragingly that the Small Person stopped before her.

"If you please," she said, "isn't that a new baby?"

She felt herself quite red in the face at her temerity, and

"IS IT A VERY NEW ONE?" THEY ASKED.

there was no doubt an honest imploring in her eyes, for the lady smiled again.

"Yes," she answered. "Do you want to look at it?"

"Oh, yes, please," they both chimed at once. "We do so love them."

The baby's face was covered with a white lace veil. The lady bent toward them, and lifting it, revealed the charms beneath.

"There," she said.

And they gasped with joy and cried together:

"Oh, isn't it a *beautiful* one!" though it was exactly like all the others, having neither hair, features, nor complexion.

"Is it a *very* new one?" they asked. "*How* new?" And their hearts were rejoiced with the information that it was as new as could possibly be compatible with its being allowed to breathe the air of Heaven.

In reflecting upon the conduct of this elderly person—who was probably a sort of superior monthly nurse—I have always felt obliged to class her with the jocular Park police-man who, in the buoyancy of his spirits, caused the blood of the Small Person to congeal in her infancy by the sprightly information that she would be taken to prison if she fell on the grass through the back of the seat.

This lady also regarded the innocence of tender years as an amusing thing. Though how—with the adoring velvet eyes of the Best Friend fixed trustingly on her, and with the round face of the Small Person burning with excited delight as she talked—it was quite possible for her to play her comedy with entire composure, I do not find it easy to explain.

"Are you so very fond of babies?" she inquired.

"We love them better than anything in the world."

"Better than dolls?"

"Oh, thousands better!" exclaimed the Small Person.

"But dolls don't cry," said the stranger.

"If I had a baby," the Small Person protested. "it wouldn't cry, because I should take such care of it."

"Would you like a baby of your own?"

I feel sure the round face must have become scarlet.

"I would give worlds and worlds for one!" with a lavishness quite unbiassed by the limits of possession.

The stranger was allowing the friends to walk slowly by her, one on either side. In this way there seemed to be established some relationship with the baby.

"Would you like me to give you this one?" she asked, quite seriously.

"*Give* it to me?" breathless. "Oh, you *couldn't*."

"I think I could, if you would be sure to take care of it."

"Oh, oh!" with rapturous incredulity. "But its Mamma wouldn't let you!"

"Yes, I think she would," said the lady, with reflective composure. "You see, she has enough of them!"

The Small Person gasped! Enough of new babies? There was a riotous splendour in such a suggestion which seemed incredible. She could not help being guilty of the rudeness of regarding the strange lady, in private, with doubt. She was capable of believing almost anything else—but not that.

"Ah!" she sighed, "you—you're making fun of me."

"No," replied this unprincipled elderly person, "I am not at all. They are very tiresome when there are a great many of them." She spoke as if they were fleas. "What would you do with this one if I gave it to you?"

At this thrilling suggestion the Small Person quite lost her head.

"I would wash it every morning," she said, her words tumbling over each other in her desire to prove her fitness for the boon. "I would wash it in warm water in a little bath and with a big soft sponge and Windsor soap—and I would puff it all over with powder—and dress it and undress it—and put it to sleep and walk it about the room—and trot it on my knees—and give it milk."

"It takes a great deal of milk," said the wicked elderly person, who was revelling in an orgy of jocular crime.

"I would ask Mamma to let me take it from the milkman. I'm sure she would, I would give it as much as it wanted, and it would sleep with me, and I would buy it a rattle, and——"

"I see you know how to take care of it," said the respectable criminal. "You shall have it!"

"But how can its Mamma *spare* it?" asked the small victim, fearfully. "Are you *sure* she could spare it?"

"Oh, yes, she can spare it. Of course I must take it back to her to-night and tell her you want it, and I have promised it to you; but to-morrow evening you can have it."

Since the dawning of the Children's Century young things

have become much better able to defend themselves, in the
sense of being less easily imposed on. I believe that only an
English child, and a child brought up in the English nursery
of that period, could have been sufficiently unsophisticated to
believe this Machiavelian Monthly Nurse. In that day one's
private reverence for and confidence in the grown-up person
were things which dominated existence. A grown-up person
represented such knowledge and dignity and power. People
who could crush you to the earth by telling you that you were
" a rude little girl," or " an impertinent child," and who
could send you to bed, or give you extra lessons, or deprive
you of your pudding at dinner, wore an air of omnipotence.
To suggest that a grown-up person—" a grown-up lady " or
gentleman, could " tell a story," would have been sheer
iconoclasm. And to doubt the veracity of a respectable
elderly person entrusted with a new baby would have been
worse than sacrilegious. The two friends did not leave her
side until she left the Square to take the baby home, and
when she went all details had been arranged between them,
and Heaven itself seemed to have opened.

The next evening, at precisely a quarter-past seven, the
two were to go to the corner of a certain street, and there
they would find the elderly person with the new baby and a
bundle of its clothes, which were to be handed over with
ceremony to the new proprietor.

It was to the Small Person the baby was to be given,
though in the glow of generous joy and affection it was an

understood thing between them that the Best Friend was to be a partner in the blissful enterprise.

How did they live through the next day ? How did they learn their lessons ? How could they pin themselves down to geography and grammar and the multiplication table ? The Small Person's brain reeled, and new babies swam before her eyes. She felt as if the wooden form she sat on were a species of throne.

Momentarily she had been brought down to earth by the fact that, when she had gone to her Mamma, glowing and exalted from the interview with the elderly person, she had found herself confronting doubt as to the seriousness of that lady's intentions.

"My dear child," said her Mamma, smiling at her radiant little countenance, "she did not mean it! she was only joking !"

"Oh, *no !*" the Small Person insisted. "She was *quite* in earnest, Mamma ! She really was ! She did not laugh the least bit. And she was such a nice lady—and the baby was such a beautiful little new one ! I asked her if she was laughing at me, and she said, ' No, she was not.' And I asked her if the baby's Mamma could spare it, and she said she thought she could, because she had enough of them. She was such a *kind* lady."

Somehow she felt that her Mamma and the governess were not convinced, but she was too much excited, and there was too much exaltation in her mood to allow of her being really

discouraged, at least until *after* the fateful hour of appoint-
ment. Before that hour arrived she and her friend were at
the corner of the street which had been named.

" It's rather a common street, isn't it ? " the two said to
each other. " It was funny that she should tell us to come
to a back street. That baby could not live here, of course,
and neither could she. I wonder why she didn't bring it
back into the Square."

It was decidedly a back street—being a sort of continuation
of the one whose row of cottages the Small Person could see
from the Nursery window. It was out of the question that
the baby could belong to such a neighbourhood. The houses
were factory people's cottages—the kind of houses where
domestic differences were settled with the fire-irons.

The two children walked up and down, talking in excited
under-tones. Perhaps she had mentioned this street because
it was near the Square ; perhaps she lived on the Crescent,
which was not far off; perhaps she was afraid it would be
troublesome to carry the baby and the bundle at the same
time, and this corner was nearer than the Square itself.

They walked up and down in earnest faith. Nothing would
have induced them to lose sight of the corner for a second.
They confined themselves and their promenade to a distance
of about ten yards. They went backward and forward like
squirrels in a cage.

Every ten minutes they consulted together as to who could
pluck up the courage to ask some passer-by the time. The

passers-by were all back street people. Sometimes they did
not know the time, but at last the children found out that
the quarter-past seven was passed.

"Perhaps the baby was asleep," said one of them. "And
she had to wait until it wakened up before she could put on
its bonnet and cloak."

So they walked up and down again.

"Mamma said she wasn't in earnest," said the Small
Person ; "but she *was*, wasn't she, Annie ? "

"Oh ! yes," said Annie. "She didn't laugh the least bit
when she talked."

"The house at the corner is a *little* nicer than the others,"
the Small Person suggested. "Perhaps it is very nice inside. Do you think she *might* live there ? If she did we
could knock at the door and tell her we are here."

But the house was really not possible. She must live
somewhere else—with that baby.

It seemed as if they had walked for hours, and talked for
months, and reasoned for years, when they were startled by
the booming, regular sound of a church clock.

"That's St. Philip's bell," exclaimed the Small Person.
"What is it striking ? "

They stood still and counted.

"One-two-three-four-five-six-seven-eight."

The two friends looked at each other blankly.

"Do you think," they exclaimed, simultaneously, "she
isn't coming ? "

" But—but she *said* she would," said the Small Person, with desperate hopefulness. If she didn't come it would be a *story !* "

" Yes," said the Best Friend, " she would have told a *story !* "

This seemed an infamy impossible and disrespectful to contemplate. It was so impossible that they braced themselves and began to walk up and down again. Perhaps they had made some mistake—there had been some misunderstanding about the time—the corner—the street—anything but the honourable intentions of the elderly person.

They tried to comfort each other—to be sustained. They talked, they walked, they watched—until St. Philip's clock boomed half-past eight. Their bedtime was really eight o'clock. They had stayed out half an hour beyond it. They dared stay no longer. They stopped their walk on the fated corner itself and looked into each other's eyes.

" She *hasn't* come ! " they said, unconscious of the obviousness of the remark.

" She *said* she would," repeated the Small Person.

" It must be the wrong corner," said the Best Friend.

" It must be," replied the Small Person, desolately. "Or the baby's mamma couldn't spare it. It was such a beautiful baby—perhaps she *could not !* "

" And the lady did not like to come and tell us," said the Best Friend. " Perhaps we shall see her in the Square again some time."

" Perhaps we shall," said the Small Person, dolefully. It's too late to stay out any longer. Let us go home."

They went home sadder but not much wiser little girls. They did not realize that the respectable elderly person had had a delightful, relatable joke at the expense of their inno-cent little maternal souls.

Evening after evening they walked the Square together watching. But they never saw the new baby again, or the sardonic elderly female who carried it.

It is only a thing not far away from Paradise—not yet acclimatized to earth—who can so trustingly believe and be so far befooled.

CHAPTER VII.

THE SECRÉTAIRE.

WONDER why it was called the Secrétaire? Perhaps it had resources the Small Person never knew of. It looked like a large old-fashioned mahogany book-case, with a big drawer which formed a ledge, and with a cupboard below. Until she was seven or eight years old she did not " discover " the Secrétaire. She knew that it existed, of course, but she did not know what its values were. She used to look at its rows and rows of books and sigh, because she knew they were " grown-up books " and she thought there was nothing in them which could interest her.

They were such substantially bound and serious-looking books. No one could have suspected them of containing stories—at least, no inexperienced inspector. There were rows of volumes called " The Encyclopædia," rows of stout volumes of *Blackwood's Magazine*, a row of poets, a row of miscellaneous things with unprepossessing bindings, and two rows of exceedingly ugly brown books, which might easily have been suspected of being arithmetics, only that it was of course incredible that any human creature, however lost, could have been guilty of the unseemly brutality of buying arithmetics by the dozen.

The Small Person used to look at them sometimes with hopeless, hungry eyes. It seemed so horribly wicked that there should be shelves of books—shelves full of them—which offered nothing to a starving creature. She was a starving creature in those days, with a positively wolfish appetite for books, though no one knew about it or understood the anguish of its gnawings. It must be plainly stated that her longings were not for " improving " books. The cultivation she gained in those days was gained quite unconsciously, through the workings of a sort of rabies with which she had been infected from birth. At three years old she had begun a life-long chase after the Story. She may have begun it earlier, but my clear recollections seem to date from Herod, the King, to whom her third year introduced her through the medium of the speckled Testament.

In those days, I think, the Children's Century had not begun. Children were not regarded as embryo intellects, whose growth it is the pleasure and duty of intelligent maturity to foster and protect. Morals and manners were attended to, desperate efforts were made to conquer their natural disinclination to wash their hands and faces, it was a time-honoured custom to tell them to " make less noise," and I think everybody knelt down in his night-gown and said his prayers every night and morning. I wish I knew who

was the originator of the nursery verse which was a kind of
creed :—

> " Speak when you're spoken to,
> Come when you're called,
> Shut the door after you,
> And do as you're told."

The rhyme and metre were, perhaps, not faultless, but the
sentiments were without a flaw.

A perfectly normal child knew what happened in its own
nursery and the nurseries of its cousins and juvenile friends ;
it knew something of the romances of Mrs. Barbauld and
Miss Edgeworth, and the adventures related in Peter Parley's
" Annual." Religious aunts possibly gave it horrible little
books containing memoirs of dreadful children who died early
of complicated diseases, whose lingering developments they
enlivened by giving unlimited moral advice and instruction to
their parents and immediate relatives, seeming, figuratively
speaking, to implore them to " go and do likewise," and
perishing to appropriate texts. The Small Person suffered
keen private pangs of conscience, and thought she was a
wicked child, because she did not like those books and had a
vague feeling of disbelief in the children. It seemed probable
that she might be sent to perdition and devoured by fire and
brimstone because of this irreligious indifference, but she
could not overcome it. But I am afraid the Small Person
was not a normal child. Still she really could not help it,
and she has been sufficiently punished, poor thing, even
while she has been unduly rewarded. She happened to be

born, as a clever but revoltingly candid and practical medical man once told her, with a cerebral tumour of the Imagination.

Little girls did not revel in sumptuous libraries then. Books were birthday or Christmas presents, and were read and re-read, and lent to other little girls as a great favour.

The Small Person's chase after the Story was to assume the proportions of a crime.

"Have you any books you could lend me?" she always ended by asking a new acquaintance.

"That child has a book again!" she used to hear annoyed voices exclaim, when being sent up or down stairs, on some errand, she found something to read on the way, and fell through the tempter. It was so positively unavoidable and inevitable that one should forget, and sink down on the stairs somewhere to tear the contents out of the heart of a few pages, and it was so horrible, and made one's heart leap and thump so guiltily, when one heard the voice, and realized how bad, and idle, and thoughtless, and disobedient one was.

It was like being conquered by a craving for drink or opium. It was being a story-maniac.

It made her rude, too, and it was an awful thing to be rude! She was a well-mannered enough child, but when she went to play with a friend in a strange nursery, or sitting-room, how was it possible to resist just *looking* at a book lying on a table? Figure to yourself a beautiful, violently crimson, or purple, or green book, ornamented with gorgeous, flaring designs in gilt, and with a seductive title in gilt letters on the back, and imagine how it could be possible that it should not fill one's veins with fever.

If people had just understood and had allowed her to take such books and gallop through them without restraint. (She always galloped through her books, she could not read them with reasonable calmness.) But it was rude to want to read when people want to talk or play with you, and so one could only breathlessly lift a corner of a leaf and devour half a dozen words during some momentary relief from the other person's eye. And it was torment. And notwithstanding her sufferings, she knew that it was her fate to be frequently discussed among her friends as a little girl who was rude enough " to read when she comes to see you."

As she did not develop with years into an entirely unintelligent or unthinking person, there may lie a shade of encouragement to anxious parents in the fact that she was not conscious of any thirst for " improving " reading. She wanted stories—any kind of stories—every kind—anything from a romance to a newspaper anecdote. She was a simple, omnivorous creature. She had no precocious views about her mind or her intellectual condition. She reflected no more on her mind than she did on her plump legs and arms—not so much, because they were frequently made red and smarting by the English east winds—and it did not occur to her that she had an intellectual condition. She went to school because all little girls did, and she learned her lessons because only in that manner could she obtain release at twelve in the morning and four in the afternoon.   She seemed always to know how to read, and spelling had no difficulties for her; she rather liked geography, she thought grammar dull, and she abhorred arithmetic.   Roman and Grecian and English history, up to the times of the Georges, she was very fond of. They were the Story she was in chase of.   Gods and goddesses, legends and wars, Druids and ancient Britons, painted blue, worshipping in their groves, and fighting with their clubs and spears against the splendid Romans in their chariots—these fed the wolf which gnawed her innocent vitals.   The poor, half-savage Briton, walking in wonder through the marvellous city of his captors, and saying mournfully, "How could you who have all this splendour wish to conquer and take from me such a poor country as mine?"—this touched her heart.   Boadicea the Queen was somehow a wild, beautiful, majestic figure—Canute upon the sea-shore, commanding the sea to recede, provided the drama—and Alfred, wandering in the forest, and burning the cakes in the neat-herd's hut, was comedy and tragedy at once, as his kinghood stood rebuked before the scolding woman, ignorant of his power.   Henry the Eighth, Elizabeth and Bloody Mary, Richard Cœur de Lion, Richard the Third, and the poor little Princes in the Tower—one could read their stories again and again; but where the Georges began romance seemed to fade away, and the Small Person was guilty of the base treason of being very

slightly interested in the reign of Her Most Gracious Majesty
the Queen.

"I don't care about the coal and cotton reigns," she said.
"They are not interesting. Nothing happens." Lemprière's
"Classical Dictionary" was a treasure to be clutched at any
moment—to keep in a convenient corner of the desk, so that,
when one put one's head under the lid to look for pens or
pencils, one could snatch just one scrap of a legend about a
god or a goddess changed into something as a punishment or
to escape somebody or other.

Remembering these ill-satisfied hungers, her own childhood
being a thing of the past, and the childhood of young things
of her own waiting for its future, she gave them books as she
gave them food, and found it worthy of note that, having
literature as daily bread and all within reach before them, they
chose the "improving" things of their own free will. It
interested her to ponder on the question of whether it was
because they were never starving and ravenous, or that
instruction of to-day is made interesting, or whether they
were by nature more intelligent than herself.

It was an indescribably dreary day when she discovered
the gold mine in the Secrétaire. I have a theory that no one
can really know how dreary a rainy day can be until they
have spent one in an English manufacturing town. She did
not live at Seedley at that time, and as in her recollections of
the Back Garden of Eden the sun always seemed to have
been shining on roses and apple blossoms, in Islington

Square it seemed always to be raining on stone pavements
and slate roofs shining with the wet. One did not judge of
the weather by looking at the sky. The sky was generally
grey when it was not filled with dirty but beautiful woolly-
white clouds, with small patches of deep blue between. It
was the custom to judge what was happening by looking at
the slates on the roofs. There seemed to be such lots of
slates to look out at when one went to a window.

"The slates are quite wet!" was the awful sentence which
doomed to despair many a plan of pleasure. They were
always wet on the days when one was to be taken somewhere
to do something interesting.

Everything was wet on the day when she found the gold
mine. When she went to the Nursery window (the Nursery
being a back room on the third story) she looked down on
the flags of wet back yards—her own back yard and those of
the neighbours. Manchester back yards are never beautiful
or enlivening, but when the flagstones are dark and shining,
when moisture makes dingier the always dingy whitewashed
walls, and the rain splashes on their coping, they wear an
aspect to discourage the soul. The back yards of the houses
of the Square were divided by a long flagged passage from the
back yards of the smaller houses in what was called a "back
street." From the Nursery one looked down on their roofs
and chimneys and was provided with a depressing area of
wet slates. It was not a cheering outlook.

The view from the Sitting-room was no more inspiring and

was more limited. It was on the ground floor and at the back also, and only saw the wet flagstones. She tried it and retired. The Drawing-room looked out on a large square expanse of gravel enclosed by houses whose smoke-begrimed faces stared at one with blank, wet window eyes which made one low-spirited beyond compare. She tried that also, and breaking down under it, crept upstairs. It was in a room above the Drawing-room that the Secrétaire had its place, and it was on turning in despair from the window there, that her eye fell upon its rows of uninviting-looking books.

Before that particular window there was a chair, and it was a habit of hers to go and kneel by it with her elbows on its seat and her chin on her hands while she looked at the clouds.

This was because through all her earlier years she had a queer sense of nearness to the sky and of companionship with the clouds when she looked up at them. When they were fleecy and beautiful and floated in the blue, she imagined them part of a wonderful country, and fancied herself running and climbing over them. When there was only a dull lead-coloured expanse, she used to talk to it in a whisper, expostulating, arguing, imploring. And this she did that day.

"Oh!" she whispered, "do open and let me see some blue, please do! If you *please*. You can do it if you like You *might* do it! I would do it for you if I was a sky. Just

a piece of blue and some sun—just an island of blue! Do!
Do! Do!"

But it would not and did not. The rain came drizzling
down and the slates became wetter and wetter. It was
deadly—deadly dull.

The Nursery Sofa, the Green Arm Chair, the very Doll
itself seemed to have the life taken out of them. The Doll
sat in her chair in the Nursery and glared in a glassy-eyed
way into space. She was nobody at all but a Doll. Mary
Queen of Scots, Evangeline, and the Aztec royalties seemed
myriads of miles away from her. They were in the Fourth
Dimension of Space. She was stuffed with sawdust, her nose
was a blunt dab of wax, her arms were green kid, her legs
dangled, her toes turned in and she wore an idiotic wig.
How could a Small Person " pretend " with a thing like that?
And the slates were wet—wet—wet! She rose from her
kneeling posture before the chair and wandered across the
room toward the Secrétaire, to stare up at the books.

" I wish I had something to read ! " she said, wofully. " I
wish there was something for me to read in the Secrétaire.
But they are just a lot of fat, grown-up books."

The bound volumes of *Blackwood's Magazine* always
seemed specially annoying to her, because there were bits of
red in the binding which might have suggested liveliness.
But " Blackwood's Magazine " ! What a title ! Not a hope
of a story in that. At that period cheerfulness in binding
seemed to promise something, and the title did the rest.

But she had reached the climax of childish *ennui*. Something must be done to help her to endure it.

She stared for a few moments, and then went to another part of the room for a chair. It must have been heavy for her, because English chairs of mahogany were not trifles. She dragged, or pulled, or carried it over to the Secrétaire. She climbed on it, and from there climbed on to the ledge, which seemed at a serious distance from the floor. Her short legs hung dangling as she sat, and she was very conscious that she should tumble off if she were not careful. But at last she managed to open one of the glass doors, and then, with the aid of cautious movement, the other one. And then she began to examine the books. There were a few —just a few—with lively bindings, and of course these were the first she took down. There was one in most alluring pale blue and gold. It was called, " The Keepsake," or " The Garland," or " The Floral Tribute," or something of that order. When she opened it she found it contained verses and pictures. The verses were beautifully printed plaints about ladies' eyes and people's hearts. There were references to " marble brows," and " snowy bosoms," and " ruby lips," but somehow these charms seemed to ramble aimlessly through the lines, and never collect themselves together and form a person one could be interested or see a story in. The Small Person feverishly chased the Story through pages of them, but she never came within hailing distance of it. Even the pictures did not seem real. They were engravings of wonderful ladies with smooth shoulders, from which rather boisterous zephyrs seemed to be snatching airily flying scarves. They all had large eyes, high foreheads, exceedingly arched eyebrows, and ringlets, and the gentleman who wrote the verses about them mentioned an ardent wish to " touch his lute " in their praise. Their Christian names were always written under them, and nobody ever was guilty of anything less Byronic than Leonora, or Zuleika, or Haidee, or Ione, or Irene. This seemed quite natural to the Small Person, as it would really have been impossible to imagine any one of them being called Jane, or Sarah, or Mary Anne. They did not look like it. But, also, they did not look like a story.

The Small Person simply hated them as she realized what fraudulent pretences they were. They filled her with loathing and rage.

She was capable of strange, silent, uncontrollable rages over certain things. The baffled chase after the Story was one of them. She felt red and hot when she thrust back the blue and gold book into its place.

" You are a Beast ! " she murmured. " A Beast—Beast—Beast ! You look as if you were something to read—and you're nothing ! "

It would have been a pleasure to her to kick the Keepsake all over the room, and dance on it. But it was her Mamma's book. The next pretty binding contained something of the same kind. It enclosed the " Countess of Blessington," the

" Hon. Mrs. Norton," and " L. E. L." The first two ladies did not interest her, because they looked too much like the Eudoras and Irenes, but somehow L. E. L. caused her to pause. It seemed curious that a young lady should be called L. E. L., but there was something attractive in her picture. She was a slender little young lady in a white muslin frock and a very big belt and buckle, and there was something soft and prettily dreamy in her small face. The Small Person did not know why she looked like a real creature, and made one feel vaguely sad, but it was very thrilling to discover later that she was like Alice Benbolt—that she also had been part of a sort of story—and that, like Alice, she

" lay under the stone."

It was when she had been put back on the shelf that the Small Person was driven to take down a volume of *Blackwood*.

I wonder how much depended upon her taking down that particular volume. I am more than inclined to think that it was absolutely necessary that she should have things to read. I am also aware that no one knew how fierce her childish longings were, and it would have occurred to nobody about her that she had any longings unfulfilled at all, unless it was a desire for more " sweeties " than would have been good for her. The kindly, gentle people who loved her and took care of her thought Peter Parley's " Annual " enough for any little boy or girl.

Why not? It was the juvenile literature provided for that day, and many children throve on it. She was not an intellectually fevered-looking Small Person at all. She was a plump, red-cheeked little girl, who played vigorously, and had a perfect appetite for oatmeal porridge, roast mutton, and rice-pudding.

And yet I can imagine that, under some circumstances, a small, imperfect, growing thing, devoured by some rage of hunger it cannot reason about or understand, and which is for ever unsatisfied, might, through its cravings, develop some physical fever which might end by stilling the ever-working brain. But this may only be the fancy of an imaginative mind.

The *Blackwood* was a big book and heavy. She opened it on her knee—and it opened at a Story !

She knew it was a story, because there were so many short lines. That meant conversation—she called it "talking." If you saw solid blocks of printed lines, it was not very promising, but if you saw short lines and broken spaces, that meant "talking"—and you had your Story.

Why do I remember no more of that story than that it was about a desolate moorland with an unused, half-forgotten well on it, and that a gentleman—(who cannot have been a very interesting character, as he is not remembered clearly) —being considered superfluous by somebody, was disposed of and thrown into it in the *rôle* of a Body ? It was his body which was interesting, and not himself, and my impression is that the story was not specially fascinating—but it was a Story, and if there was one in the fat volumes there must be others—and the explorer looked with gloating eyes at the *rows* of fat volumes—two whole rows of them!

She took down others, and opening them, saw with joy more "talking." There were stories in all of them—some which seemed to be continued from month to month. There was a long one called "The Diary of a Physician," another called "Ten Thousand a Year"—this last, she gathered in a few glances, contained the history of a person called Tittlebat Titmouse—and was about a beautiful Kate Aubrey, and her virtuous but unfortunate family—and about a certain Lady Cecilia—and, oh! the rapture of it!

Her cheeks grew hotter and hotter, she read fast and furiously. She forgot that she was perched on the ledge, and that her legs dangled, and that she might fall. She was perched in Paradise—she had no legs—she could not fall. No one could fall from a Secrétaire filled with books, which might all of them contain Stories!

Before long she climbed up and knelt upon the ledge so that she could be face to face with her treasures, and reach even to the upper shelves. With beating heart she took down volumes that were not *Blackwood's,* in the wild hope that even they might contain riches also. She was an excitable creature, and her hands trembled as she opened them. Across a lifetime I remember that her breath came quickly, and she had a queer feeling in her chest. There were books full of poetry, and, oh, Heaven, the poems seemed to be stories too ! There was a thing about an Ancient Mariner with a glittering eye, another about St. Agnes's Eve, another about a Scotch gentleman called Marmion, others about some Fire Worshippers, a Peri at the gate of Eden, a Veiled Prophet, a Corsair, and a splendid long one about a young man whose name was Don Juan. And then a very stout book with plays in it, in queer old-fashioned English. Plays were stories. There were stories about persons called " Othello," " The Merchant of Venice," " Two Gentlemen of Verona," " Romeo and Juliet," and a world of others. She gasped with joy. It would take *months* to finish them !

It was so tragic to finish a book.

" I wish I had something to read," she used to say often.

" Where is that book I saw you with yesterday ? "

" I've finished it," she used to answer, rather sheepishly, because she knew they would reply :

" Then you can't have read it properly. You couldn't have finished it in such a short time. You must skip. Read it again."

Who wanted to read a thing again when a hunger for novelty was in them ?

The top row of the shelves looked so unpromising that she was almost afraid to spoil the happiness by touching the books.

They looked ancient and very like arithmetics. They were bound in ugly greyish boards with a strip of brown down the back.

She pulled herself up to read the titles. They all seemed to belong to one edition. The one her eyes seized on first was quite a shabby one.

"The Fair Maid of Perth," she read. "Waverley Novels."

Novels were stories! "The Fair Maid of Perth." She snatched it from its place, she sat on the ledge once more with her feet dangling. "The Fair Maid of Perth." And all the rest were like it! Why, one might read *forever!*

Were the slates still wet? Was the gravelled Square still sopping? Did the flagged pavement still shine? Was the Doll still staring in her chair—nothing but a Sawdust Thing?

She knew nothing about any of them. Her feet dangled, her small face burned, she bounded to Perth with the Fair Maid. How long afterward a certain big bell rang, she did not know. She did not hear it. She heard nothing until a nursery maid came in and brought her back to earth.

"You naughty girl, Miss Frances. The tea-bell's rung and you sitting here on your ma's Secretary—with a book!"

She gathered herself together and scrambled off the ledge. She went down to tea, and the thick slices of bread and butter deemed suitable to early youth—but she had the grey and brown volume under her arm.

The governess looked at her with the cold eye of dignity and displeasure.

"You have a book," she said. "Put it down. You are not allowed to read at table. It is very rude."

CHAPTER VIII.

THE PARTY.

HE Christmas holidays were a time of great
festivity, and they began with the "Breaking-
up." The "Breaking-up" was a magnificent
function, and was the opening and event of
the season.

"We're going to break up in two weeks," little girls of
different schools said to each other ; "when are *you* going to
break up?"

The Breaking-up was a delightful ending of the school
days, and the rapturous beginning of the holidays, and it
was properly celebrated by a party given by the ladies who
were the proprietresses of the school.

It was a glorious social event, looked forward to through
all the year, but it was not entirely given up to the frivolous
caperings of emancipated youth. It had, indeed, a
utilitarian significance and importance in the minds of the
hostesses. It was, in fact, not all cakes and ale, though
cakes were plentiful and ale—in the form of negus and
lemonade—flowed freely.

Not only the "young ladies and gentlemen" of the scholastic establishment were invited, but Mammas and Papas, and it was the Mammas and Papas who were the serious feature of the entertainment. The Papas did not always appear, but no Mamma was ever absent unless subdued by mortal illness. Nothing less would have kept one away. Papas were deterred by much less serious reasons.

Only an ex-pupil, chastened by the seriousness of years, could possibly describe the splendour of the scene. Until thus chastened, his adjectives would get the better of him.

Something magic was done to the entire establishment, which gave it a beautiful, awe-inspiring air of not being the same house, and of having nothing whatever to do with lessons; in fact, with anything at all but approaching holidays. Carpets were taken up, furniture was moved from one place to another, or whisked out of sight when it was in the way. Holly was hung and wreathed about pictures, there were pink and white paper roses, and from the centre of the ceiling of the transformed drawing-room there hung candidly a fine piece of mistletoe. Round this room, against the wall, sat the Mammas and such stray Papas as had been overcome by a sense of paternal duty or by domestic discipline. The Mammas were always attired in their most imposing frocks. They were frocks about which there was nothing frivolous—black, or grey, or purple, or brown silks or satins; and if they wore caps—which they usually did—

their caps were splendid.   My impression is that the English
mamma of that day dressed at twenty as she did at fifty,
and that gaiety and youth expressed themselves merely in
caps, which ventured on white lace, and pink or blue ribbon,
instead of black lace and purple or dark red.   All Mammas
appeared the same age to the Small Person, and were alike
regarded with the reverence due to declining years.   They
formed an imposing phalanx at the " Breaking-up."

" What are you going to wear at the Party ? " every little
girl asked every other little girl some time during the
weeks before the festal occasion.

What one wore was an exceedingly brief white, or pink,
or blue, or mauve frock, exceedingly beautiful stockings,
exceedingly new slippers, and an exceedingly splendid sash
—and one's hair was " done " in the most magnificent way.
Some had crimps, some had curls, some had ribbons, some
had round combs.   The Small Person had rows and rows
of curls, and a round comb to keep them out of her eyes.

The little boys had Eton jackets, broad and spotless
collars, and beautiful blue and red bows for neckties.   It
was also the fashionable thing for the straight-haired ones
to be resplendently curled by the hairdresser, which gave a
finishing touch to their impressively shining and gala air.

The pink and blue and white frocks and sashes only
added to the elated delight of the little girls, I am sure.
They enjoyed their slippers and tiny white kid gloves (they
had only one button then), and were excited by their little

lockets and necklaces, but I do not think the boys enjoyed their collars and new jackets, or ever forgot that their hair had been curled, until they reached the supper-room and were handed oranges and tipsy-cake.

But these exhilarations were not reached until the serious business of the evening was over. It was very serious to the Small Person. She disliked it definitely, and never felt that the " Breaking-up " had begun until her share of it was over. To walk into the middle of the room, to make one's most finished little curtsey, and then, standing, surrounded by a circle of Mammas in their best caps, to " say a piece of poetry," was not an agreeable thing. I do not think her performance ever distinguished itself by any special dramatic intelligence. I know she was always devoutly glad when it was over and she could make the final curtsey and hastily retire. She also felt the same sense of relief when she had struck the last chord of the show " piece " she was expected to play upon the piano, and reached the last note of her exhibition song. When one reflects that each music pupil was called upon for a like performance, and that numberless careful recitations were given, it is, perhaps, not unnatural that Papas were not plentiful. But not a Mamma flinched.

But after all this was over the Christmas Holidays had begun. The short frocks and sashes danced quadrilles and round dances with the Eton jackets and spotless broad collars. There was a Christmas-tree in the school-room and upon and beneath it were such prizes as meritorious efforts had gained for accomplishments or good conduct. In the dining-room there were sandwiches and cake and oranges, and crackers with mottoes within expressive of deep and tender emotions. One jumped very much when they went off, and the daring exchanged mottoes with each other. Cowslip wine flowed freely, and there was negus with bits of lemon floating in it—in fact, one felt one's self absorbed in the whirling vortex of society, and wondered how grown-up people, to whom Parties were comparatively every-day affairs, could possibly walk calmly on the surface of the earth. The Breaking-up was a glittering—a brilliant thing.

And it was only the beginning.

All through the three weeks' holiday there were other entertainments almost as brilliant. They would have been quite as brilliant only that they were not the Breaking-up. Every little boy or girl, whose Mamma could indulge in such a luxury, gave a Christmas Party. They were all called Christmas Parties during these holidays. And through all these festivities the Small Person was conscious of a curious fatality which pursued her, and which is perhaps worth recording because it was a thing so human, though she did not in the least comprehend its significance.

Each time that a note arrived "hoping to have the pleasure" of her company—and that of her sisters and brothers—wild exhilaration reigned. Everybody began to be excited at once. A party seemed a thing it was impossible to wait patiently for. It got into one's head and one's body, and made one dance about instead of walking. I do not think this resulted from anticipation of the polkas and games or the negus and tipsy-cake, or was absolutely a consequence of the prospect of donning the white frock and sash and slippers—it was the Party that did it. Perhaps young birds who have just learned to fly, young ducks in their first plunge into a pond, young chanticleers who have discovered they can crow, may feel something of the same elation and delight. It was the Party!

And when such eventful evenings arrived what a scene the Nursery presented! How intoxicating the toilette was—from the bath to the snapping of the clasp of the necklace which was the final touch! How one danced about, and broke into involuntary outbursts of romps with one's sisters! How impossible it was to stand still while one's hair was curled, and how the poor nurse and governess reproached, reasoned, implored for decorum, and at intervals appealed to one's Mamma, who came in intending to restore order with a word, and entering amid the chaos of frocks and sashes and unbridled rapture, was overwhelmed by its innocent uncontrollableness, and said, without any real severity at all:

"Now, *children!* You really *must* be quiet and let yourselves be dressed! You will *never* be ready for the Party!"

The last awful possibility usually restored order for a few seconds, but it was impossible that it should last long. Nature was too much for one.

The picture of the Nursery on such occasions is one of those which remain to me. The bright fire, which danced itself, the numberless small garments scattered about, the Party frocks whose sacredness entitled them to places apart

THE THREE UNRESTRAINABLE SMALL PERSONS IN VARIOUS STAGES OF UNDRESS.

which seemed quite like Altars, the sashes lying on top of them, the three unrestrainable small persons darting about in various stages of undress, the nurse pursuing them with a view to securing buttons or putting on slippers, the mirror in which one saw reflected an excited, glorified Party face, with large, dancing eyes, and round cheeks which were no other shade than crimson or scarlet.   These are the details.

But the clasp of the necklace snapped at last, the small white glove was buttoned, the small wrap enfolded one's splendour, and the minute after one was rolling through the streets, going to the Party.

And then one was standing upon the steps and the front door was opened, revealing a glittering scene within, where numberless muslin or tarlatan frocks and Eton Jackets passed up and down the enchanted staircase, or hesitated shyly until some hospitable person took charge of their timidity.

To-day—even in the manufacturing towns in England— the entertainments given to youth are probably not of a nature as substantial as they were then.   They were not matters of mere ices and fruits and salads then.   By no means.   The Small Person herself, who was the proprietor of a noble and well-rounded appetite, was frequently conscious of staggering a little under the civilities of hospitality. The sad, the tragic truth which is the sting of life—that one can have Enough, and that after it one wants no more— more than once touched her with a shade of gentle, though unconsciously significant, melancholy.   She realized no occult illustration and thought it a mere matter of cakes.

First there was tea.   One sat with all the Party at long tables.   There were very buttery muffins and crumpets and Sally-lunns, and preserves and jellies and marmalade, and currant cake, and potted shrimps and potted beef, and thin bread-and-butter and toast, and tea and coffee, and biscuits, and one was asked to eat them all, whether one was capable of it or not.

"Have another piece of muffin, dear," the mamma of the occasion would say, with pressing bounteousness. "Oh, come, you *must*, love—just one piece—and some more strawberry jam; you have not made a good tea at all. Jane," to the parlour-maid, "muffins and strawberry jam for Miss Frances." And her voice was always so amiable, and it was so hard to persist in saying, "No, thank you, Mrs. Jones," with all the Party looking on, that one tried again until it could only have been through a special intervention of Providence that appalling consequences did not ensue. And then when that was over one went into the drawing-room, which was decorated with holly and mistletoe, and where the Party Frocks and Eton Jackets at first exhibited a tendency to fight shy of each other and collect in polite little groups until somebody grown up interfered and made them dance quadrilles or play "Hunt the Slipper" or "Old Soldier." After that they began to enjoy themselves. They were not precociously conventional young persons. His first awkwardness worn off, the Eton Jacket had no hesitation in crossing the floor to the particular White Frock seeming desirable to him.

"Will you dance this waltz with me?" he would say. Upon which the White Frock would either reply:

"Yes, I will," or, "I've promised Jemmy Dawson," in

which latter case the Eton Jacket cheerfully went and invited somebody else.

There were a great many polkas and schottisches. These, in fact, were rather the popular dances. They were considered better fun than quadrilles. The Party danced them until it became quite hot, and the Eton Jackets were constrained to apply handkerchiefs to their heated brows. To subdue this heat and sustain exhausted nature, trays of lemonade and negus and oranges and little cakes appeared, borne by servant - maids in Party caps with ribbons. It was not supposed that a Party could subsist on air — and supper would not be announced until nearly eleven. The oranges were cut in quarters

"WILL YOU DANCE THIS WALTZ WITH ME?"

and halves so that they might be easily managed, the negus was usually in a resplendent bowl with a ladle in it.

Then the dancing began again and there were more games and the festivities became more and more brilliant. The White Frocks whirled about with the Eton Jackets, they were candidly embraced under the mistletoe, the grown-up people looked on and commented upon them in undertones and

sometimes laughed a great deal.   Sometimes in dancing past
a group one heard some one say, "Emmy dances very well,"
or "How pretty Marian is!" or "Very fine boy, Jack
Leslie!" And if one were Emmy or Marian or Jack one
blushed and tried to look as if one had not heard.

It was generally in the midst of this whirl of frocks and
sashes, the gay strains of the dance-music, the chattering,
laughing voices, that the Small Person found herself beset by
that fatality which has been referred to. It was a curious
thought which gave her a sense of restlessness she did not
like.

She was very fond of dancing. She was an excitable Small
Person, and the movement, the music, the rhythm of it all
exalted her greatly. She was never tired and was much
given to entering into agreements with other White Frocks
and Eton Jackets to see which could outdance the other. It
was an exciting thing to do. One danced until one's cheeks
were scarlet and one's heart beat, but one never gave up
until some one in authority interfered.

Having stopped—laughing and panting and standing with
her hand against her little side as she watched the kaleido-
scopic whirl, the music and voices and laughter filling her
ears, she so often found she was asking herself a question,
"Is *this* the Party?"

It seemed as if something in her insisted on realizing that
the joy looked forward to with such excitement had absolutely
materialized.

"Is this *really* the Party?" she would say mentally. And then, to convince herself, to make it real, "Yes, this is the *Party*. I am at the *Party*. I have my Party frock on—they are all dancing. This is the Party."

And yet as she stood and stared, and the gay sashes floated by, she was restlessly conscious of not being quite convinced and satisfied, and of something which was saying,

"Yes—we are all here. It looks real, but somehow it doesn't seem exactly as if it was the *Party*."

And one does it all one's life. Everybody dances, everybody hears the music, everybody some time wears a sash and a necklace and watches other White Frocks whirling by—but was there ever any one who really went to the Party?

CHAPTER IX.

THE WEDDING.

 "GROWN-UP young lady" was a very wonderful being. She wore a long frock, sometimes with numbers of flounces, she went to church in a bonnet made of tulle and flowers, or velvet and little plumes, she had rings on, and possessed a watch and chain. It was thrilling to contemplate her from afar. It seemed impossible that one could ever attain such dazzling eminence one's self. She went to Balls. No one knew what a Ball was, but it was supposed to be a specially magnificent and glorified kind of Party. At Balls grown-up gentlemen in dress suits, and with rare flowers in their buttonholes, danced with the young ladies who wore ethereal dresses, and perhaps wreaths, and who carried bouquets. These resplendent and regal beings talked to each other. One did not know what they talked about, but one was sure that their conversation was at once sparkling, polished, and intellectual beyond measure, something like grammar, geography, and arithmetic set with jewels of noble sentiment and brilliant repartee. Only the most careful application to the study of one's lessons, one's morals, and one's manners could fit one to presume to think that in coming ages one might aspire to mingle with such society.

The proprietresses of the school at which the Small Person spent her early educational years were young ladies. But no one in the school would have been irreverent enough to realize this. Representing as they did education, authority, information of the vastest, and experience of the most mature dignity, one could not connect the insignificance of youth with them. One of them was perhaps twenty-three, the other twenty-four or five, and though neither wore caps, and both wore ringlets, as the Mammas all seemed of equal age, so these two young ladies seemed to be of ripe years. One day, indeed, there was a grave discussion among the little girls as to what age these dignified persons had attained, and one of them heard it.

She was really a rounded, sparkling-eyed, rather Hebe-like little creature, with a profusion of wonderful black ringlets. It was the hour of ringlets.

"And how old do you *think* I am?" she inquired, of one of her pupils.

She was looking at them from behind her table, with rather amused eyes, and suddenly the Small Person who was regarding her became subtly conscious of a feeling that it was possible that she *was* younger than the Mammas. "How old?" said the girl who had been asked. "Well—I should think—of course I don't know, but I should *think*—about forty.

It was interesting but seemed rather unnatural that their friends and companions seemed to be *real* young ladies. Was it possible that there were real young ladies whose recreation consisted in talking about Roman emperors, the boundaries of Europe, the date when Richard I. began to reign, Lindley Murray's impressions on the subject of personal pronouns and the result of the " coming over " of William the Conqueror ? Could it be that when they took tea together they liked to be asked suddenly " Who was the first King of all England ? " or " What is Macclesfield noted for ? " or " Where are the Oural Mountains ? '

It seemed as if it would be more than human nature could endure to have such delicate questions as these pressed and dwelt upon, in combination with muffins and thin bread-and-butter, but what else *could* they talk about ? Uneducated flippancies were impossible.

A faint suggestion of other possibilities was shadowed forth in the imaginative mind of the Small Person by her introduction one day to two pink silk dresses. They were shown to her by the little sister of the two teachers, and they were to be worn by these sedate persons to a Ball.

The ladies were the elder daughters of one of the *un*widowed gentlemen in reduced circumstances. He had begun life as a presumable heir to an old estate and fortune. Fate had played him a curious trick which disinherited him, and ended in his living in the Square, and in his daughters keeping a " select seminary for young ladies and gentlemen."

But they had relatives on whom Fate had not played tricks, and there were some young ladies in beautiful little bonnets, who were their cousins, and who came to see them in a carriage, and were considered radiant.

" The carriage from Grantham Hall is standing before the Hatleigh's door," some child would announce to another. " Let us go and walk past. It is Miss Eliza who is in it, and you know she's the prettiest. She has a lavender silk frock on and a lace parasol."

There were legends of marvellous enjoyments at Grantham Hall. Perhaps they were all results of the imaginations of tender years, but they continually floated in the air. Perhaps the younger sisters were rather proud of the possession of cousins who went to Balls and had such bonnets.

But it is a fact without doubt that the two pink silk frocks were preparation for some gala event at Grantham.

The Best Friend was one of the younger sisters (their name was legion), and it was she who first imparted to the Small Person the thrilling confidence that Sister and Janey had each a beautiful pink frock to wear at the party at Grantham.

" They are both lying on the bed in the spare bedroom," said the Best Friend. " The party is to-night, and they are all ready to put on. I wish Sister would let me take you in to look at them."

The little lady who was supposed to be forty was always called " Sister." She was the eldest of a family of nine.

On being appealed to she was sufficiently indulgent to give permission to the Best Friend to exhibit the festal glories.

So the Small Person was taken into the spare bedroom. It was no trivial incident. The two pink silk frocks lay upon the bed, the waiting wings of two brilliant butterflies, at the moment setting copies in a chrysalis state. They had numberless tiny flounces "pinked out" in lovely little scallops round the edge, they had short puffs for sleeves, and they . had low bodices with berthas of

THE TWO PINK SILK FROCKS LAY UPON THE BED.

tulle and tiny rosebuds around them.

The Small Person positively blushed with admiration and

rapture. How *could* Sister, being attired in a thing like this, lift her dark eyes to the grown-up gentleman waltzing with her and say to him, with proper firmness :

" Fifteen from fifty-seven and how many remain ? "

The Small Person felt it would be impossible, though she knew nothing whatever of the circumstances under which it was not impossible for a very bold grown-up gentleman to say :

" My charming Sister, my education has been neglected, but if you will give me the fifty-seven and permit me to take the fifteen away, I will endeavour to calculate."

It might easily have been Sister and Janey who were the principal features of the two marriages which were the first nuptial ceremonies appearing upon the stage of the Small Person's existence. But it was two of the cousins who were the brides—two of the young ladies from Grantham Hall.

Rumours of the approaching ceremonies being whispered in the schoolroom, the most thrilling interest was awakened. The prospect was more exciting than the Breaking-up itself. There was something at once festive and imposing about it. Opinions as to the nature of the ceremony were numerous and varied. No one had ever attended a wedding, and yet somehow nearly every one could supply some detailed information.

Whispered conversation on the subject could not be wholly repressed, even by authority. From some mysterious reliable source it was ascertained that the principal features of the sacred contract were that the grown-up young lady wore a singularly resplendent and ethereal white frock, that she was wreathed with orange-blossoms and adorned with a white veil accompanied by a splendid bouquet and a grown-up gentleman. The grown-up gentleman was not dwelt upon particularly; one always asked of the bride, "Is she pretty?" but nobody ever inquired if he was pretty. He seemed immaterial, so to speak, and when not slurred over he seemed somehow to be regarded with some slight vague distrust.

Every pupil knew what the bride was going to be dressed in, what her veil was made of, what flowers were to compose her bouquet, but no interest whatever was felt in the possible costume of the grown-up gentleman.

The Small Person, while interested in him as a mystery, was conscious that he was regarded as a sort of necessary flaw in the occasion. The Story gave him interest to her. She had never seen him, but recollections of Ernest Maltravers, Quentin Durward, and the Master of Ravenswood gave him a nebulous form. The wedding was to be a double one, the two sisters being married at once, consequently there were two grown-up gentlemen involved, and it was rather soul-stirring to hear a vague rumour that one of them—who was very handsome, having dark eyes and a straight nose—was not smiled upon by the bride's papa, and that he had forced his way to the altar through serious parental opposition.

He was not considered a sufficiently staid and well-to-do grown-up gentleman. There were suggestions of the Master of Ravenswood in this.

"I wonder if they like each other very much?" this sentimental little Person rather timidly inquired.

But no one seemed to know anything beautiful and romantic about it, so she combined with his straight nose and dark eyes the misfortunes and attributes of all the heroes in the "Secrétaire," and found it thrilling that he was on the point of leading to the shrine the veil and the orange-blossoms, and thus being made happy for ever after.

What a morning it was when the wedding took place. There were no lessons. The two young teachers were to be among the bridesmaids. They were to wear veils and wreaths themselves, and several of the most decorous little girls were going to the church to look at them. They went in a body, attired in their best frocks and feeling quite light-headed with their exalted sense of anticipation.

The sun was shining brilliantly, everything was shining brilliantly one felt. The cabs and omnibuses seemed to rattle by with a gay, rather reckless air, the passers-by moved more briskly than usual, in fact there was in the atmosphere a suggestion that everybody and everything must be going to a wedding. Everybody of course must know about it and be interested, indeed there were evidences of interest in the fact that as people passed by they nearly always glanced at the open church door, and a few rather shabby persons having loitered about the entrance, their number continued adding to itself until they formed a waiting group.

The Small Person and her companions waited also. Nobody could have thought of going into the church until the carriages had arrived and they had seen everybody get out, not to mention the fact that being inexperienced they were timid and lacked the courage to take any bold steps. They stood very much in awe of an official in a sort of gown who was known as the "Parroter," and whose function it was to show people to pews on Sunday and look pained and annoyed when little boys sneezed too frequently or dropped things.

"Perhaps the 'Parroter' wouldn't let us in," said someone. "Dare you ask him?"

But nobody dared do anything until the bridal party arrived. It seemed as if it would never come. The waiting in the street seemed to last hours and hours, and was filled with tumultuous agitations caused by false alarms that the carriages were coming.

"Here they are!   Here they are!" somebody would cry. "I'm sure that's a carriage turning the corner down the street.   Don't you see it?"   And then every one became elated and moved nervously for fear she had not a good place, and pulses quickened and hearts beat—and the carriage probably turned out to be a cab.   They wandered up and down restlessly to make the time pass more quickly, and one or two bold spirits even went and peeped into the church, but

retired precipitately at the approach of the "Parroter." The
Small Person—after what appeared to her some sixteen hours
of suspense and agitation—was pervaded by an awful secret
fear that at the last moment Quentinravenswoodmaltravers
had been for ever tabooed by his bride's family and there
would be no wedding at all.

But at last, at last the bells began to ring that loud, gay,
hilarious wedding-chime, the bell-notes seeming to race and
tumble over each other in their hurry to be joyful.

There was something curiously intoxicating about it. It
was the Party over again—only more than the Party. The
Small Person looked up at the bell-tower and the blue sky
behind it. What exquisite blue sky! What soft little fleecy
white clouds! What a beautiful day! "Happy is the bride
that the sun shines on." Some one had said that, and the
sun was shining! The carriages were there and the crowd
about her were stirring with excited curiosity. But she saw
only vaporous whiteness and flowers and dowager's rich
colours, with blots of grown-up gentlemen. The sun was
shining, the bells were chiming, the church was filling.
Happy was the bride that the sun shone on. But all brides
were happy! The sun always shone on them. What a
strange, delightful, exalting event it was to be married!

She never knew how she was led or dragged or hustled
into the church. Some other little girl more practical and
executive than herself managed her. But presently she was
there, ensconced in a high pew in the cathedral greyness.

The church was a cathedral and impressed her deeply. She felt religious and wondered if she ought not to say her prayers. She was not calm enough to see detail—she was too emotional a Small Person, and this was the first time she had seen any one married. The vaporous whiteness, the floating veils and flowers were grouped about the altar, the minister seemed to be taking the brides and the grown-up gentlemen to task at some length. He called them Dearly Beloved, but appeared to address rather severe warnings to them. The Small Person had a vague feeling that he was of the opinion that they would come to a bad end if not admonished in time. She hoped they would not—particularly Quentinravenswoodmaltravers, whose straight nose she had been too deeply moved to single out from the rest. For a moment or so she felt that it was so solemn to be married that it was almost conducive to low spirits. But she cheered up after the minister appeared to have relented and let them off and they moved away to the vestry. Then there was a stir among the spectators, which soon became a bustle, and she was led or dragged or hustled out into the sunshine and renewed joyous clangour of the bells.

There was a great bustle outside. The crowd of lookers-on had increased, and a policeman was keeping it back, while the carriages stood in line and closed up one by one as the floating frocks and veils, and dowagers' velvets and satins, and blots of grown-up gentlemen filled them, and were driven away. The Small Person watched it all as in a dream.

The bells raced and clamoured, the sun shone brighter than ever. She was only a Small Person who had really nothing to do with these splendours and who no more contemplated the magnificent prospect of being married herself than she contemplated being crowned in Westminster Abbey. Such glories as these were only for grown-up people. But they were beautiful—beautiful!

The young ladies who had been married—in full panoply of white satin and wreaths and veils—were each handed into a carriage by the grown-up gentleman they belonged to, who got into the carriage also.

After they had all driven away, the bells had ceased their clamour, and the crowd dispersed, one sharp-eyed little person made a most interesting statement:

"I saw in as their carriage drove past," she announced, "and he had Miss Grantham's head on his shoulder."

"Which one was it?" inquired the Small Person. She was *sure* it was Quentinravenswoodmaltravers.

And inquiry proved that it was.

CHAPTER X.

THE STRANGE THING.

IT seems inevitable that each individual, in looking back to childhood and the school-room, should recall distinct memories of certain children who somehow stood out from among their fellows, made prominent or set apart a little by some beauty, strength, or cleverness, or some unattractiveness or disability. There is, perhaps, in every school-room, the girl or boy who is handsome, who has fine eyes or splendid hair, the one who learns lessons with amazing quickness, the one who is specially well-dressed and has an air of well-being, the one who is dull or common-looking, the one who *is* somehow commoner than any one else, the one who has an easy, fearless manner, and is suspected of being the " favourite " of those in authority, the one, poor child, who is physically ugly and unpleasant, and cannot rise against the fate which has treated him so cruelly.

The Small Person knew each of these types. She was not consciously an aristocratic little Person, but she had an intense, silent dislike to, and impatience of, the " common " ones. She found them antipathetic to a degree which was trying, as one of them happened to be amusing and another really good-natured. She continually tried to adjust herself to them, but the " commonness " always interfered. It made the good-natured one ridiculous and the amusing one odious and unprincipled. Among the younger ones there was a little boy who impressed her without actually being interesting. He was not clever, he was not pretty, he was not engaging. He was an inoffensive little fellow, and set apart in her imagination by a mysterious unfortunateness. As I look back I think it possible that he was really a shy and gentle little fellow, on whom one's maturity might look with great tenderness. The Small Person felt a vague kindliness for him, though she was not at all intimate with him.

" He is very delicate," people said of him, and she could not but regard him with a sort of curiousness. She was not delicate, no one belonging to her was delicate. She belonged to a family of romping, red-blooded creatures, and the idea of being " delicate " seemed mysterious as well as mournful.

And he had such a strange, unnatural look. He was slight and insignificant, light-haired and grey-eyed, and he had a peculiarity marked among the groups of plump and rosy juveniles about him—instead of being pink or rose-coloured, his cheeks and lips were bluish purple. They were distinctly far from the normal colour. They were not red at all, and sometimes they looked quite violet.

"What a queer colour Alfie's lips are," was often said. "Isn't it funny! They're blue, and so are his cheeks."

And then some one would say wisely, and rather proud of the superior knowledge :

' It's because he has heart disease. I heard Miss Janey speaking about it. He may die quite suddenly."

And then some one would know stories of people who had died suddenly, and would relate them, and a sense of awe would pervade everybody, as it always did when Death was spoken of—though it was so impossible, so *impossible* that any of themselves could die. People did die, of course, people who had lived to be quite old, or who had caught scarlet fever in some phenomenal way, but somehow they seemed to belong to a world quite far off and quite different to the one in which one's self lived—to the world of the Nursery and the Square, and the School-room where one did one's sums wrong and could not remember the date of Henry VIII.'s marriage with Anne Boleyn. Oh, no, that would be too incongruous !

It gave the Small Person a curious feeling to try to realize that the plain, quiet little boy with the blue lips might *die*— *die* quite suddenly. Once she gave him a new slate-pencil because of it, though she did not tell him why, and was perhaps scarcely definite herself about it. She used to forget her geography in looking at him questioningly when he did not see her.

It must have been one of the "common" ones who one morning came to her, wearing an air of excited elation in her consciousness of having startling news to impart, and who greeted her with—

" Have you heard about Alfie Burns ? "

" No," she answered, " what about him ? "

" He's *dead*," said the news-bearer. " He wasn't at school yesterday—and he died this morning."

So the Strange Thing came among them into the school-room—among the forms and desks and battered books, making itself in an unreal way as real as the ink-stands and slate-pencils. It had come to Alfie Burns, with his little ordinary face and lank hair, and yet it still remained *impossible*. It had come to Alfie Burns—but it could not come to any of the rest of them. Somehow he must have been " different." He was " delicate " and had that queer colour. At any rate he was " different " now, and seemed impossible too. There was a curious intense craving for detail among the older ones. Every one wanted to know *how* he had died, and if he had *said* anything. In the books of memoirs the little boy or girl always said " last words," which were a sort of final scriptural or instructive effort. They were usually like this :

" Father," said James, between his paroxysms of agony, " try to be a better man, that you may meet me in Heaven."

" Brother Thomas," said Mary Ann, faintly, " do as Mother tells you, and obey your Sabbath-school teacher."

" Please do not swear any more, Uncle William Henry," said little Jane, as her mother wiped the death-damp from her brow. "I shall be in Heaven in a few minutes, and I want you to come."

Remembering these things one wondered what Alfie's "last words" had been. It would have seemed almost impossible that any one could die without last words. Wicked people always expired in frightful torment, using profane language or crying for mercy or writhing with remorse because they had not been better before they were taken ill. Alfie had been a sort of indefinite, insignificant little boy. He was not naughty, but his goodness had a passive negative quality, and he never reproved or instructed any one. So it was difficult to adjust one's self to the situation, and imagine how the Strange Thing would find him when it came.

And nobody knew any detail. There seemed to be none. He had died, and of course it was supposable that his parents had cried, and we knew he would be buried. And though the event was discussed and discussed from all points of view, this was all any one knew.

No one had ever been to his house or seen his parents. They were quiet business people who did not belong to the Square, and, as far as the school seemed to know, he had no brothers or sisters, and must have had a rather dull life. He did not seem to have any particular companions or to invite people to his house to play or to have tea with him.

According to all orthodox beliefs—and in an innocent way nothing could have been more orthodox than all the school— he had gone to Heaven and was an Angel.

This the Small Person found a tremendous problem to grasp. I know that it pervaded her for days, and I wonder why she did not talk about it to somebody grown up. Perhaps it was her infant English habit of reserving her sentiments and emotions, combined with her secret consciousness that she was so little and that the grown-up people were so big that they could not really understand one another's point of view. Of course to people who knew all about Death and Heaven and Angels her remarks would seem silly and trivial—perhaps even disrespectful. She did not ask anything, but was oppressed and permeated by a vague sadness and sense of unexplained things.

Heaven was a place without laws or boundaries. Anything could be done there—if one once got in—and everything was there. There was a Great White Throne, there were streets of gold, and walls built of " all manner of precious stones." The stones she remembered principally were the chalcedony and sardonyx, sardius, chrysolite, beryl, and chrysoprasus, because they had strange names, and she wondered what colour they were. And there was a Woman on a " scarlet-coloured beast, full of names of blasphemy, having seven heads and ten horns," and though she was in Heaven she was " drunken with the blood of the saints." And there were Dragons and Beasts, and there were Elders and Pale Horses and Golden Candlesticks and Golden Vials. And the Beasts were full of eyes before and behind and had six wings each, and the horses had breast-plates of fire and jacinth and brimstone, and heads of lions, and fire and smoke came out of their mouths. It was all in Revelations, and so it was true. Heaven was like that, and Alfie Burns had gone there —out of the school-room and the atmosphere of ink-stands and copy-books, from making mistakes in his sums, and cleaning his slate with an unsavoury " slate-rag " or sponge, from looking yearningly out at the other slates on the roofs to see if it was raining, and there was no prospect of playing. And now suddenly he was an Angel and wore wings. Wings seemed as impossible as the Strange Thing which had happened to him. It was so difficult to adjust them to his little blue-lipped face and small insignificant figure which his clothes seemed always rather too large for.

" But he would be quite different," the Small Person persisted obstinately to herself as her only consolation. " He would be quite different, and he would be dressed in white robes."

The draperies she tried to see him in were something of the nature of a very voluminous, very white night-gown— but at all events they were " quite different." The interest of all this is that what we begin with at seven we seem to end with at seventy. How are we less vague—what more do we know ? Nothing—nothing—nothing, but that, whatever it is—wherever it is—it is " quite different."

In the years which lie between we have learned more geography, more astronomy ; we have learned that the blue is space, and the clouds are vapour ; but what more definite, but that we clamour for something, we plead for something, we *must* have something, we *ought* to have something " quite different."

Somebody—probably it was the executive, practical little girl, who had had the energy and ability to hustle the vague Small Person into the church at the Grantham wedding—somebody proposed that two or three select ones should go to Alfie's home and ask to be allowed to " see " him.

The Small Person was awed. She wanted very much to see him—what was left of him after he had become an angel. " His soul has gone to Heaven, his body is only dust," that was what was always said. She somehow wanted to look at the poor little body which was only dust.

" Perhaps we oughtn't to go," she said, timorously. " Perhaps they won't like us to see him."

But she was taken. Somebody else had been and nobody had seemed to dislike their going. The Small Person, I have frequently reflected, was always *taken* to places. She was not a strong Small Person, except in unsuspected powers of keeping quiet under some strong emotions, and in possessing a certain silent steadiness of purpose when she meant to do a thing. Perhaps her strength was and always has been that she quite unconsciously looked as if she meant nothing while she really meant a great deal. But that was probably far less a moral or mental quality than a gift amiably bestowed by Nature in a lavish moment. The leading spirits took her to the place under their charge. Afterward she did not seem to remember anything about the house, even its entrance or stairway—anything but a certain dull, dreary little front parlour in it. This was most likely because she remembered the little dismal room and what was there so strangely well.

It was such a dull, unpicturesque room, small and un-adorned, and dreary beyond measure. At least, so it seemed to the Small Person, though she saw no detail of it but a stiff horsehair-covered sofa against a wall. On this sofa lay something covered with a white sheet. This was what they had come to see. Somehow the room, the sofa, the whole atmosphere of the colourless dulness seemed like the little unornamental fellow himself, with his lank hair, his ill-fitted clothes, and his mild, small, unattractive, bluish face. The person who had taken charge of them drew the white sheet away, and the Small Person saw the Strange Thing for the first time, with an awful sense of desolateness and depression.

Even the Strange Thing had not left the poor little fellow beautiful. He seemed to have grown very long; he was clothed in an awesome garment of bluish white flannel, with ornamentation of ugly stamped scalloped edges; in accordance with some belated gruesome fashion he had on a strange muslin night-cap whose stiff crimped frill border made an unlovely setting for his poor little still, bluish face. It looked more dusky than ever in its strange blue colour, and his lips were almost violet. A line of lifeless grey showed itself under the not entirely closed lids.

The Small Person stood and looked down at this with a

rather awful feeling. She did not know what she had expected to see, but this made her heart beat with dreary throbs. It was not that she was exactly frightened ; on the whole she was not as frightened as she had expected to be when she came face to face with the Strange Thing, but she felt an indescribable awed dreariness. She also wondered why she did not begin to cry. She had imagined that at the sight of the Strange Thing one would inevitably begin to cry. She wondered if it was because she had no heart that she did not. Ought one really to sob bitterly at the sight of a little boy one had not known at all well, and of whom one chiefly remembered that he had heart disease and blue lips.

"He is an Angel," she kept insisting, mentally. "He has gone to Heaven."

The girl who had taken her to the house whispered to her, telling her to touch him. She had touched him herself, and so had the others. This appeared to be part of a ceremony. The Small Person shrank very much. She felt that it would be an awful thing to do. And yet she had heard so much about a certain strange coldness—colder than anything else —not the same thing as any other coldness—as "cold as Death." There was a fearsome longing to know what it was like. And if one touched what the Strange Thing had left, one did not dream about it. One could not bear the thought of dreaming of the small room, the horsehair sofa, and the poor little unlovely object with the frilled muslin cap and eyelids not quite closed.

She put out her hand and touched the unsmiling cheek.

"As cold as Death!" It was not as cold as she had imagined it would be. Not as cold as ice or as cold as snow —and yet—and yet—it was unlike anything else—a soft chillness which somehow seemed to hold no possibility of its

SHE PUT OUT HER HAND AND TOUCHED THE UNSMILING CHEEK.

ever being warmed. What she carried away from the dreary little room when she left it, was the memory of that soft chillness and a sort of wonder at herself, because she had really seen the Strange Thing.

"Poor little Alfie," the executive child said. "I am very

sorry for him, but he's better off." The general opinion expressed was that everybody was " sorry " for him. It would have been unfeeling not to be sorry. There was also the greatest possible stress laid on the fact that he had gone to Heaven, and these sentiments were regarded as so incontrovertibly proper, that it would have occurred to no one to find their connection incompatible. Curious as it may seem, I do not remember that the Small Person herself did.

An unquestioning acceptance of all axioms was the feature of the period, and she was so full of the mystery of the Strange Thing itself, that she could contemplate nothing less, though she knew that she gained nothing by contemplating that.

But though she had seen it, and so had the others ; though they had looked down at its rigidity, and touched its coldness with their warm hands ; though it had come into their very midst—to Alfie Burns, who was nobody particular, and who had played and done his sums wrong just like the rest of them—they knew it could not come to any of themselves ; they did not say so, of course, but they were quite secure in it, and were not afraid at all.

For the Small Person, perhaps, it was well that it was not very long before it came again. I do not know how long ; but the second time it wore another face, and was touching but not gruesome. And it was better to see, that it might be so, than to remember always the grimness of the ugly, dreary room—better for any one ; far, far better for a child with a vivid mind.

In the school there was a department for younger children, quite little ones, who learned their alphabet and played Kindergarten games. They had a room of their own and a teacher of their own. There were some attractive mites among them, and " the older ones," as the others called themselves with a feeling of great maturity, had favourites and pets.

There was a tiny one who was the pet of all—such a pretty pet and such a laughing one ! She was three years old and had golden-brown eyes and little nut-brown curls on her small round head. She was a merry thing, full of dimples, and her brown-gold eyes were large and love-compelling, and had long curling lashes. The child pet of a school full of girls is a much loved thing. This one was adored. Her lovers never tired of praising her prettiness, her quaint little movements, her eyelashes, her curls and eyes. She was a little lovely one, and her tiny name was Selina.

" Look at her ! " everyone would exclaim when a Kinder-garten game was being played. " Oh, see how pretty she is when she puts her teenty elbow on her knee and leans her cheek on her hand to show how the labourer rests. She keeps opening her eyes and laughing. She can't keep them shut."

This very game was played on Friday afternoon, and she was at her very prettiest and quaintest. Earlier in the day, it was remembered afterward, she had been a little dull and had not seemed quite herself, but in the afternoon she had brilliant rose-coloured cheeks, and her merry eyes were like stars.

"Isn't she a sweetie?" said the girls. "Isn't she a little rogue? Look at her peeping under her eyelashes."

When the Small Person came to school on Monday morning the door was opened for her by one of the elder girls of the family. She had a curious shocked look in her eyes.

"Has any one told you?" she exclaimed. "Have you heard about it?"

"Heard what?" the Small Person faltered, startled by her expression.

"Little Selina is dead! Pretty little Selina!"

And so the Strange Thing came again!

This time the difficulty was to *believe* it—to feel that it *could* be true.

"Little Selina!" the Small Person gasped. "She—she *can't* be! Who told you? On Friday she was playing the Haymaker game and she kept peeping—she could not keep her eyes shut—and we laughed so! *Selina!*"

"It's quite true," was the answer. "She was ill then, though she had such red cheeks. Janey said she hadn't seemed bright in the morning. They say she hadn't been quite herself for a day or so. She died at six this morning, and they sent word by a servant. She *was* crying, poor girl!"

What a Strange Thing it was !

In the school-room the children looked at each other
amazed. They were *amazed*—that was it. Each new-comer
uttered the same exclamation, "Selina?" and then "*Selina!*"
As if it were too incredible. They kept telling each other
how merry she had been when she played the Haymaker
game, how rosy her cheeks had looked, how roguishly she
had laughed. They kept repeating that she was such a pretty
little thing and everybody loved her. And somehow there
was a tendency even in the common ones to look bewildered
and thoughtful, and exclaim, in a puzzled, questioning undertone, " Selina ?   *Selina !* "

The Small Person found she was saying it to herself all
through the day. It had seemed extraordinary that Alfie
should be taken away, even though they had all known about
the heart disease. It had been extraordinary because the
Strange Thing seemed to have nothing to do with such people
as themselves—to be only possible to people somehow quite
remote and unlike them. But there seemed a reason why
Selina should not be taken, the reason of *herself*, her pretty,
buoyant, dimpling, vivid self. What had the awful thing to
do with that ? It was unnatural.

" Selina ?   *Selina !* "

I think it was the velvet-eyed little Best Friend and her
younger sister who went with the Small Person to the child's
home, to see her, as they had seen Alfie. It was the first
time they had ever been to the house. The children saw

very little of each other away from the school-room, and
Selina only appeared on the small horizon when her nurse
brought her to the front door and left her to pursue her tiny
studies.

Of this house, also, the Small Person never remembered
anything afterward but one room, which has remained a
picture hung in the gallery of life.

It was not a large room. It was a nursery bedroom,
perhaps, though there was no bed in it, only a little cot
standing in the middle of it, and prettily draped in white.

Everything in the room was white, covered with pure
white, hung with white, adorned with white flowers—mostly
white rosebuds—very tender little ones. It seemed like a
little chapel of snow, where one felt one must breathe softly.

And under the snowy draperies of the small cot, among
rosebuds which seemed to kiss it with their petals, there was
another little white thing lying.

Selina? *Selina!*

Ah, little love! how pretty and innocent and still the
Strange Thing had left her. It could not have hurt her.
She was not changed, only that she was somehow lovelier.
There were rosebuds in her hands, and on her pillow; her
eyelashes looked very long as they lay upon her cheek, and
in a still, strange little way she was smiling. In the white
room, among the white flowers, looking down at her fair child-
sleep through tears, one was not the least afraid.

The Small Person was vaguely glad of something, and somehow she knew that she was not "sorry for her." She looked, and looked, and looked again, with tenderly brooding eyes. She did not want to go away. If the Strange Thing only left one a soft, white creature in a white room, among flowers,

AND SHE BENT OVER AND KISSED HER ROUND CHEEK.

and smiling like that, at what it had showed one, it was not so awful. What a pretty, pretty smile—as if she was keeping a little secret to herself.

"May we kiss her?" the Small Person asked, in a low voice, timidly.

" Yes, dear," was the answer.

And she bent over and kissed her round cheek where the dimples used to play. And the coldness was only the soft coldness of a flower.

And afterward they went away, talking together in low, tender, child whispers. And they told each other again what a pretty little thing she had been, and that everybody had loved her. And the Small Person remembered how in the game she had made everybody laugh, because she could not keep still, and could not keep her eyes closed. But now--now, she was quite still, and she could keep her pretty eyes shut.

And this had been done by the Strange Thing.

CHAPTER XI.

" MAMMA "—AND THE FIRST ONE.

THE chief tone of her world was given to it by the gentle little lady who was her mother—the most kind and simple English lady—of a type the most ingenuous and mild. What the Small Person felt most clearly was that " Mamma " was so entirely and sweetly this gentle and kindly *lady*. Of course it had not been necessary to formulate this, even in thought, but it was an existent fact which made life pleasant. One could not have borne existence—even as a Small Person —if one's " Mamma " had not been a lady. There were Mammas who were not quite so nice—who wore more ribbons in their caps and who could be seen at a greater distance, and who had not such soft voices, and such almost timidly kind smiles and words for every one. The Small Person was always thankful after interviews with such Mammas that her own was the one who belonged to her, and to whom she belonged.

It was so interesting to hear of the days when she had been a little girl also.

" When I was a little girl and we lived at Patricroft——"
was the slender link which formed a chain of many dear
little stories of quite another world.

She had not been Romantic. The Small Person had a
vague feeling that she herself might have been the subject of
memoirs of a sweet and not awe-inspiring kind. " Mamma "
could never have been denunciatory. She seemed a little
like Amelia Sedley, but not so given to weeping and not so
silly. There were two little water-colour pictures, which
hung in the drawing-room. They were to represent,
ideally, Amy Robsart and Jeanie Deans. They had sweet
pink faces and brown ringlets, and large, gentle blue eyes.
They were very much alike, and the Small Person was very
fond of them because Mamma had one day said : " Poor
Papa bought them before we were married because he thought
they were like me. I used to wear my hair like the picture
of Jeanie Deans."

To the Small Person this surrounded them with a halo.
The vision of " Poor Papa " overcome by youthful ardour
before he was married to Mamma, and tenderly buying these
two little pictures because they were like her, and had ringlets like hers, was simply delightful to her. How could she
help loving them ?

Was Mamma clever? No, I think not. The Small
Person never asked herself the question. That would have
been most sacrilegious unlovingness. And why should one
have thought of asking more of her than that she should be

"Mamma." One would not ask one's self if an Angel were clever. And, also, one did not think of wondering how many years she had lived. She was just the age of a mamma. Only as long as she lived her mind was like that of an innocent, serious, young girl—with a sort of maidenly

"WHAT IS IMPROVING, MAMMA?"

matronliness. Not being at all given to eloquence or continuous conversation of any sort, it was a wonderful thing that her mere existence near one meant so much — that it soothed headaches, and made sore-throats bearable; that it smoothed stormy nursery seas, and removed the rankling sting of wrong and injustice. One could have confronted any trial, supported by the presence of this little, gentle, very ingenuous and unworldly Mamma.

She was a sweetly feminine thing, and her literature had been as feminine as herself. The Small Person found out about that. She had read "improving" works when she was a young lady. She had a great respect for Miss Martineau and Mrs. Ellis and her "Daughters of England." She had read poems in Keepsakes and knew all the beauties of Dr. Watts. Mrs. Barbauld she revered, and a certain book called "Anna Lee, the Maiden, Wife, and Mother," she admired most sweetly.

"But you ought not to read tales so much," she used to say, with a gently heroic sense of maternal duty, to the Small Person. "You ought to read something Improving."

"What is Improving, Mamma?" the Small Person would reply.

Gentle little lady Mamma! I am afraid she was vague—though the Small Person did not realize that it was vagueness she always observed in her blue eye when she asked this question. The answer was always the same:

"Oh!—history and things, love. History is always improving."

The Small Person used to wonder why History particularly. It was never suggested that grammar, geography, and arithmetic were stimulating to the mind—but history always. And she knew all "Pinnock's England" and "Pinnock's Rome" and somebody else's "Greece." Could there have been in Mamma herself a lurking fondness for the Story which was not "improving"? There were three or four mentioned at different periods which she seemed to remember interesting details of with remarkable clearness. " The Scottish Chiefs," " The Children of the Abbey," " Fatherless Fanny," " The Castle of Otranto," and " The Mysteries of Udolpho." Certain incidents in them being inadvertently described to the Small Person so inflamed her imagination that the most burning desire of her life was to be the happy possessor of these rich treasures. It was years before she came upon them, one by one, and then somehow their glory had departed. The mysterious secreted relative wandering about the cloister's ruins had lost her sorrowful eerie charm, the ghastly, apparently murdered victim, concealed by the heavy curtain, had no impressiveness, and it was not really a shock when he turned out to be only wax. Emily—the beautiful persecuted Emily in " Udolpho "—was actually tedious in her persistent habit of " giving vent to her feelings in the following lines." But when Mamma told bits of them with a certain timidity engendered by their romantic lack of the element of " improvement," what thrillingly suggestive things they were !

What a beautiful thing this pure and gentle heart was— quite as simple as the heart of a child, and filled with sweetest, lenient kindness to all things ! What a beautiful thing for a little child to grow up in the mild sunshine of ! What brilliant strength could have had such power—if it had not had its sweetness too ! How did one learn from it that to be unkindly and selfish was not only base but somehow vulgar too—and that the people who were not born in the "back streets" naturally avoided these things as they avoided dropping their h's and speaking the dialect?

Nobody ever said "Noblesse oblige," nobody ever said anything about "Noblesse" at all, and yet one knew that in certain quiet, unpretentious houses the boys and girls must be "ladies and gentlemen," and to be so one must feel inadmissible some faults it was by no means difficult to fall into. There is, after all, a certain quaint dignity in the fixed quantities understood by some English minds in the words "lady" and "gentleman." The words themselves have been vulgarized, and cheapened, and covered with odd gildings and varnish, and have been made to mean so many objectionable things, that it has seemed better taste to let them drop out of fashion—but once their meaning in simple, gentle minds was something very upright and fine. They were used in this sense in the days of the Small Person—at least she believed them to mean nothing less.

In searching the past there is no memory of any lecture delivered by "Mamma" on the subject of good morals, good manners, and good taste. Anything from "Mamma" in the nature of a harangue would have seemed incongruous. Perhaps it was because through all the years *she* never was unkind or ungenerous, because she was good to everything— even to disreputable and objectionable stray cats and lost dogs brought in—with bursts of enthusiasm—for refuge; because she never uttered a vulgarly sharp or spiteful, envious word, or harboured an uncharitable thought—perhaps it was because of these things that one grew up knowing that her unspoken creed would be :

" Be kind, my dear. Try not to be thoughtless of other people. Be very respectful to people who are old, and be polite to servants and good to people who are poor. Never be rude or vulgar. Remember to be always a little lady."

It was all so simple and so quite within the bounds of what one could do. And, all summed up and weighed, the key-note of it was but one thing: "Be kind, my dear— be kind."

There was an innocent, all-embracing prayer, which the entire Nursery said unfailingly every night and morning, through all its childhood—some of them, perhaps, far beyond childhood, because of the tender homely memories it brought back. One of them, at least, in after years, when the world had grown to wider boundaries and faith was a less easy thing, found a strange, sad pleasure in saying it because its meaning was so full of trustingness, and so sweet.

Surely it was "Mamma" who was responsible for it— "Mamma" who had a faith so perfect and simple, and who, in asking for good, could have left out in her praying nothing, however poor and small.

As she grew to riper years the Small Person often pondered on it and found it touching, in its all-embracingness.

It began with the Lord's Prayer—the first words of this being said devoutly as, " Our Father, 'chart in Heaven, ' and the more *slowly* one said it all, the more devout one was supposed to be. The child who "gabbled" her prayers was "a wicked thing." It was very awful, when one was tired or preoccupied, to find out that one was "gabbling." Discovering this, one went back and began again, with exceeding deliberation.

But it was the little prayer which came after this which so took in all the world—leaving out none—in its blessing:

"God bless Papa and Mamma," it began, lovingly, "and Grandpapas and Grandmammas"—though when the Small Person first remembered it the Grandpapas were gone, and one could only say, "and Grandmammas," because the Grandpapas had "gone to Heaven," and so needed no praying for, because in Heaven everybody was happy and God took care of them without being asked every night and morning by the wearers of the little white night-gowns, by the little white beds, in the Nursery. "God bless my Brothers and Sisters," it went on, lovingly again, "and my Uncles and Aunts and Cousins." And then, that none might escape and be forgotten, "Pray God bless *all* my Relations and Friends," and then, in an outburst of sympathy, "Pray God, bless Everybody." And modestly, at the end—and with the feeling that it was really a great deal to ask—"And make Me a Good Child—for Jesus Christ's Sake. Amen."

One felt, with all one's little heart, that this could be only done "For Jesus Christ's Sake"—because one *knew* how far one was removed from the little girl who died of scarlet fever in the Memoirs.

And then one finished with three dear little verses which seemed to provide for all in one's child-life—and which remembered one's friends again, and took one even to the gates of Paradise.

In Nursery parlance it was always spoken of as " Jesus tender."

"Did you say your ' Jesus tender ? ' " was sometimes sternly demanded by one little white Night-gown of another. " You were such a little bit of a time kneeling down, if you said it you *must* have gabbled."

It was this :

> " Jesus, tender Shepherd, hear me,
>   Bless Thy little lamb to-night ;
> Through the darkness be Thou near me,
>   Keep me safe till morning light."

That seemed to make everything so safe when the gas was turned down.

> " Through the Darkness be Thou near me "—

the strange, black Dark, when anything might come out of corners, or from under the bed, or down the chimney, and if one heard a sound, one could only huddle one's head under the clothes and lie listening with beating heart. But if " Jesus tender " was there, and would keep one safe till

morning light, one need not be really afraid of anything.
And then came the little thankful part :

> " Through this day Thy hand hath led me,
>   And I thank Thee for Thy care.
>   Thou hast warmed and clothed and fed me,
>   Listen to my evening prayer."

And then the last, where the poor little sins were asked
mercy for, and the friends were embraced again, and one was
left happy—taken care of—dwelling in Paradise with the
Tender one :

> " Let my sins be all forgiven,
>   Bless the friends I love so well,
>   Take me, when I die, to Heaven,
>   Happy there with Thee to dwell.
>   For Jesus Christ's sake.   Amen."

It was very sweet and very trusting—full of belief, and full
of love and kind faith in and for all the world. And whatever of faith might fade in the glare of maturity, which
made all things too real or too vague, to say simply every
night and morning through a whole childhood, words as
confiding and as kind must be a good beginning for an
innocent life—for any life, however spent.

The First One—a development of that notable seventh
year—was written one Sunday evening in Summer, when it
was clear twilight and the church bells were ringing. She
sat at the Sitting-Room Table which for the time was merely

a table made to rest things upon. She was fond of the act
of scribbling, and frequently had filled pages in blank books
with lines of angular letter m's joined together. The doing
it gave her the feeling of writing with rapidity and ease as
older people did. There was something in the free movement of the flying pen which she liked extremely. The
long summer twilight of these Sunday evenings was always
emotionally impressive to her. She did not know why, but
that they seemed so quiet, and the house was so still, and
one did not play with the Doll or run about. She had never
been forbidden secular amusement, or talked to rigidly, but
somehow there were certain things one felt it was not exactly
proper to do on Sunday.

Sunday, in fact, was rather a nice day. After breakfast
one was dressed with such care for church. The Small
Person and her two sisters, exceedingly fresh as to frocks
and hats, and exceedingly glossy as to curls, walked to
church with Mamma and the Governess and the two brothers,
whose Eton collars presented their most unimpeachable
spotlessness.

The sermon was frequently rather long, but one did one's
best by it in the way of endeavouring to understand what it
was about. The Small Person was dissatisfied with her
character because she was conscious that her mind
frequently wandered, and that she found herself imagining
agreeable scenes of a fictitious nature. She also found that
when she checked these sinful mundane fancyings and forced

herself to strictly follow the Reverend James Jones, she was
guilty of impatient criticism, entirely unbecoming a little
girl. The literary ideal of a perfect little girl in those days
—a spotless little girl, who, being snatched away in her
youth by scarlet fever, would create quite a commotion in
Heaven by the rectitude of her conduct—was the painful
young person who had memoirs written about her, relating
the details of her sufferings and the Example she had been
to every one about her—particularly to all other children who
were not of the moral *élite* as it were. The Small Person had
extremely high standards. There was nothing she would
have been so thankful for as to find that she might attain
being an Example—and suitable for memoirs—but she had
an humble, sorrowing consciousness that such aspirations
were in vain. This was evident on the face of it. The little
girls in memoirs could not have been guilty of the vileness of
"not listening to the sermon." They heard every word of it,
and preached it over again to their companions on the way
home, by way of inspiring them to religious enthusiasm.
They never thought of *anything* but the preacher while they
were in church, and they never read anything but the Bible,
and were in the kindly habit of repeating chapters of it aloud
to people left alone with them. They always knew a text to
say when any one did anything wrong, and it always converted
the erring one upon the spot. "Thou shalt not steal," they
said solemnly, when a boy was going to steal an apple, and
he never thought of such a thing again. "Thou, God, seest

me," they said when Tommy had taken a lump of sugar, and was revelling in the crime, and he immediately put it back into the bowl—probably very much the worse for wear—but he never *looked* at the sugar-bowl again so long as he lived.

The Small Person felt she could not accomplish these things—that there was a fatal earthly flaw in her nature. Perhaps it was because she was Romantic, and no memoir had ever been written about a little girl who was Romantic. Whether it preserved them against scarlet fever or against the memoir she did not ask. But sometimes she had a sad lurking fear that if a girl out of a memoir had heard her dramatic performances with the Doll she would have said to her:

" That is *not* a bark. It is only an Arm Chair. You are not playing on a lute made of silver. You are only tooting on a tin whistle which cost a penny. You are not a gentleman. You are a little girl. And you are saying what is not true. These are all lies—and liars go to Hell."

It made her feel inclined to burst into tears when she thought of it—so she thought of it as little as possible. This may have indicated a shifty irresponsibility of nature or a philosophic discretion. She could not *live* without the Doll. She felt it sad that she was not made to be an Example, but she tried to be as unobjectionable as was compatible with her inferiority and lack of fine qualities.

And, somehow, she liked Sunday. Having had another Mamma she might have disliked it greatly, but as it existed

in her life, it had rather the air of a kind of peaceful festival.
She herself was in those days too unconscious to realize that
it combined with its spiritual calm certain mild earthly
pleasures which made an excellent foundation for its charm.
One did not go to school ; there were no lessons to learn ; the
chaos of the Nursery was reduced to order ; the whole house
looked nice and quiet ; one was so specially spotless in one's
best frock ; there was always such a nice pudding for dinner
(never rice, or bread-pudding, but something with an aspect
of novelty). For a little while after dinner one remained in
the drawing-room, and sometimes Mamma—who belonged to
the generation when " the figure " was not a matter treated
lightly, would suggest that the Small Person and her two
sisters should lie quite flat upon their backs, upon the hearth-
rug, " for fifteen minutes by the clock."

" It is very good for your backs, my dears," she would say.
" It makes them straight. It is very important that a young
lady should hold herself well. When we were girls—your
Aunt Emma and I—back-boards were used."

The Small Person quite delighted in this ceremony. It
was so nice to stretch one's plump body on the soft rug—with
the sense of its being rather a joke—and hear about the time
when people used back-boards. It appeared that there had
been schoolmistresses—genteel, extremely correct ladies who
kept boarding-schools—who had been most rigorous in insisting on the use of the back-board by their pupils. There were
anecdotes of girls who would " poke their chins forward,"

and so were constrained to wear a species of collar. There
was one collar, indeed, celebrated for certain sharp-pointed
things under the chin, which briskly reminded the young
lady when she "poked." The knowledge that scholastic and
maternal method had improved since those days, and that
one would never be called upon to use back-boards or instru-
ments suggestive of the Inquisition, was agreeable, and added
charm to lying on the rug and turning one's eyes to the ormolu
clock on the mantel every now and then, to see if the three
five minutes were gone.

After that one went for a decorous saunter round the
Square, where one always encountered the Best Friend and
her sisters, and perhaps other little girls, all in best frocks
and best hats, and inclined to agreeable conversation.

About four one returned to the drawing-room, and the event
of the day took place. Every one took a chair, and being
given an orange, disposed of it at leisure and with great but
joyful decorum, while Mamma or the Governess read aloud.

"Where did we leave off last Sunday?" the reader would
ask, turning over the leaves.

The Small Person always knew. She revelled in these
Sunday afternoons. During the rapture of their passing she
heard "Ministering Children," "The Channings," "Mrs.
Halliburton's Troubles," "Letters from Palmyra," and
"Letters from Rome," an enthralling book called "Naomi,"
which depicted dramatically the siege of Jerusalem, and divers
other "Sunday books."

Yes, Sunday was a day quite set apart, and was really very pleasant to think of. A far more brilliant woman than "Mamma" might have made it infinitely less an agreeable and bright memory. Hers was the brilliance of a sweet and tender heart which loved too kindly to give one dreary hour.

None of the younger ones went to church in the evening. "I am afraid you might be sleepy," said Mamma, which was an instance of most discreet forethought.

So not going to church, the Small Person had her evening hours in the quiet house, and liked them greatly.

The form and merits of the First One have not remained a memory, but the emotion which created it is a memory very distinct indeed. As for the creation itself, it cannot have been of any consequence but that it *was* the First One.

I see the Sitting Room with its look of Sunday neatness, the Green Arm Chair wearing a decorous air of never having braved the stormy billows, the table with its cloth quite straight upon it, and the Small Person sitting by it with pen and ink and an old exercise-book before her, the window open behind her.

The pen and ink and book were to scribble with, because it amused her to scribble. But all was so quiet around her, and the sound of the church-bells coming through the open windows was such a peaceful thing, that she sat leaning on the table, her cheek on her hand, listening to it. What is there that is so full of emotional suggestion in the sound of bells ringing in the summer twilight?   The Small Person did not know at all.   But she felt very still and happy, and as if she wanted to say or do something new, which would somehow be an expression of feeling, and goodness, and—and— she did not know at all what else.

She turned her face over her shoulder, to look at the sky, which showed over the tops of the houses in the Back Street. It was very beautiful that evening—very blue, and dappled with filmy white clouds.   It had a Sunday evening look.

After looking at it, she turned slowly to the exercise-book again—not with any particular intention, but reminded by the pen in her hand of the pleasantness of scribbling.   A delightful queer and tremendously bold idea came to her.   It was so daring that she smiled a little.

"I wonder if I could write—a piece of poetry," she said, "I believe—I'll try."

No one need ever know that she had attempted anything so audacious, and she could have the fun of trying.   There was no one in the room but the Green Arm Chair, and it could not betray her—besides the fact that it would not if it could.   It was such a nice old thing.   It had a way at times of seeming to have forgotten the adventures of its wild and rather rackety, past and of seeming to exist only to hold out its arms benignly to receive Grandmammas.   As to Pirates on the High Seas, it seemed never to have even heard of one.

A piece of poetry was a thing with short lines, and at the

end of them were words which sounded alike—which
rhymed.

> " Down on a green and shady bed
>   A modest violet grew,
>   Its stalk was bent, it hung its head
>   As if to hide from view."

> "' Charge, Chester, charge ! on, Stanley, on !'
>   Were the last words of Marmion."

> "Believe me, if all those endearing young charms
>   Which I gaze on so fondly to-day
>   Were to fleet by to-morrow and fade in these arms
>   Like fairy dreams gone to decay."

> " How doth the little busy bee
>   Improve each shining hour ;
>   It gathers honey all the day,
>   From every opening flower."

These were pieces of poetry, and they gave one something
to build on. " Bed, Head, Led, Shed—Charms, Arms, Farms,
Carms." No, Carms was not a word. Oh " Calms." And
Calms was a real word. That seemed to open up vistas. It
became quite exciting—like a sort of game. There were
words spelled differently from each other, it seemed, which
would rhyme. And the church-bells went on ringing with
that soft sound which seemed to make one think things.

What should the piece of poetry be about ? How pretty
that ringing was ! Oh, suppose one tried to write a piece of
poetry about the bells. Bells, Shells, Tells, Sells—Ring,
Sing, Fling, Wing.

And she wrote a " piece of poetry " about the church-bells, and of it there is no record whatever, but that it was the First One. How long it was before she wrote another I am not at all sure. She did not seem to rush madly on in her downward career.

Time could not possibly be calculated in those days. A month seemed to hold a Future. *Anything* might occur in the way of rapture during six weeks' holiday. If one heard that a thing would happen " Next Year," one could not feel actual interest in it. " Next century " would not have made it much less vague.

But I think she was nine or ten years old when, on another Sunday evening, she broke forth again. She had read a great deal of the " Secrétaire " by that time, and had found that in Magazines published for grown-up people there were many things to read. She had discovered that *Punch* was a source of delight, and a person of the name of Charles Dickens had attracted her attention. Perhaps the fact that she had made his acquaintance, and that she had discovered *Punch* had given a new flavour to her romanticisms. But to the last the adventures of the Doll were never clouded in their seriousness by any sense of humour. Her charm would have been lost if one could have treated her lightly, or made fun of her. *She* was Reality.

The Sunday evening when she wrote her next piece of poetry was a dark and stormy one. It was a winter evening. The rain was falling and the wind howling outside. Her sisters were in bed, every one else but one servant at church, and she was sitting in the drawing-room.

She had pen and ink before her again, without any particular reason, except that she wanted something to do, and again it was the sounds outside which gave her her impetus. There were no church-bells. They had stopped ringing long before, and the wintry storm had begun after every one must have been safely in church. It was the sound of the wind which moved her this time. It sounded all the more weird, as it rushed wailing round the houses, because she was quite alone. Sometimes it seemed to exhaust itself in sounds like mournful cries heard very far off. That particular sound had always affected her very much. When she had been a little child lying awake in the Nursery bedroom she had been heart-broken by a fancy of a baby lost in the darkness of the night and storm, and wandering alone, crying, crying for some one to find it.

This Sunday night it made her melancholy. Even the cheerful sounds of the bright fire of blazing coal were not enough to overpower the feeling. And she felt so alone that she began to wish "Mamma" and the Governess would come home from church, and wondered how they would get through the rain. It seemed lonely when the wind sounded like that.

And suddenly, as a means of distracting herself, she began to write another "piece of poetry."

It began by being a very harrowing thing. The immortal

whole was never seen by her after that night, but the flavour of the first verse was so fine that it would not be easy to for- get it. The "Secrétaire" had given her an acquaintance with more than one darkling poem, recording and immortaliz- ing the sentiments of lofty-minded persons who were the victims of accursed fate and who in the depths of their woe were capable of devoting many verses to describing their exalted scorn of things in general—particularly suns which would unfeelingly persist in shining, stars that continued heartlessly to remain bright, and skies whose inconsiderate blueness could not be too scathingly condemned. And the very loftiness of their mental altitude was the cause of their being isolated from the "hollow world." They were always "alone." Alone. That was a good idea. The piece of poetry should be called "Alone." And the wind should be heard in it. How it wailed at that particular moment. And this was the soul-stirring result :—

ALONE.

Alone—alone! The wind shrieks "Alone!"
And mocks my lonely sorrow.
"Alone—alone!" the trees seem to moan,
"For thee there's no bright to-morrow."

There were no trees—but that was immaterial. And there was no sorrow— but that also was of no consequence whatever. There was, however, a touch of unconscious realism in the suggestion of the to-morrow not wearing a cheerful aspect. The next day was Monday, and it would be necessary to go to

school again, which was a prospect never holding forth inducements of a glittering nature. She was *not* warmly attached
to school.

But the first verse really impressed her. Up to that time
I remember she had never been impressed by anything
she had done. The First One had not impressed her at
all. She had only found it very absorbing to write it. But
the tone of this struck her. It was the *tone*. It seemed
so elevated—so grown-up—so like something out of the
" Secrétaire." It suggested Lord Byron. It seemed to begin
a little like some of those things he had written about ladies
—intimating that if he was not very careful indeed they
would fall hopelessly in love with him, which might lead to
most disastrous results, but that, being the noble creature he
was, he *would* be careful, and " spare " them—which the
Small Person always thought extremely nice of him, and so
beautiful when expressed in poetry. But she had not come
to the lady in her poetry. In fact, she had not thought of
her at all, which was quite remiss, as she had imagined the
sufferer whom the wind shrieked at to be a gentleman. Perhaps such had been the feelings of Quentinravenswoodmaltravers when the eldest Miss Grantham's papa had disapproved
of him. Gentlemen in that situation, in the " Secrétaire,"
always felt that trees and things were taunting them. But
it was cheering to reflect that *he* had had a " bright to-morrow "
on the occasion when he drove home from church with the
eldest Miss Grantham's head on his shoulder.

Oh, it really was quite a beautiful piece of poetry—at least the *beginning* of it was. And she sat and gazed at it respectfully.

I have wondered since then if one has not reason to congratulate her on the thing which happened next, and on the result of it. Perhaps *Punch* and the witticisms in the grown-up magazines, and perhaps the tone of thought of the gentleman of the name of Dickens were her salvation. If it had been possible for her to write a second verse as harrowing as the first and to complete her piece of poetry with the same sentiments carried to the bitter end, this being repeated through her ripening years and giving tone to them, it seems not impossible that the effect upon her character might have been a little lowering, or at least not of the most bracing nature.

But this was what happened. Though a wildly romantic, she was a healthy and cheerful-minded Small Person, and intense as was her reverence for this first verse she found she could not *possibly* write another. She tried and tried in vain. She frowned gloomily, and listened to the wind howling. She thought of the "Corsair," and the ladies Lord Byron had "spared." She strove to depict to herself the agonies of Quentinravenswoodmaltravers before Miss Grantham's papa relented. But it was no use. She became more and more cheerful, and at last found herself giving it up with something like a giggle, because it suddenly struck her as rather funny that she was sitting there trying so hard to "think of something sorrowful."

And it occurred to her that she would try to make it into something amusing.

It is quite possible that unconscious cerebration connected with some humorous poems in *Punch* or the grown-up magazines guided her. She wrote the rest of it—and there were a number of verses—quite rapidly, and with great enjoyment. She laughed a great deal as she was doing it. It was quite a primitive and aged idea she used, but it seemed intensely amusing to her. The gentleman who had begun by being mocked and shrieked at by the wind and trees developed into an unmarried gentleman whose bachelorhood exposed him to many domestic vicissitudes and unpleasantnesses. He seemed a very hapless gentleman, indeed, and his situation was such that one did not wonder that the winds in the first verse " seemed to moan " at him, even though they intended it for another gentleman.

She finished the last verse in a burst of ecstatic low giggling. When it was all done she did not think of respecting it or admiring it at all; it did not impress her, it simply made her laugh.

I wonder if it can have really been at all actually funny. At that age one laughs so easily. I know nothing about the verses but that there was an interesting incident connected with them, and that they made some one else laugh.

Just as she finished them " Mamma " came home from church, and hearing the front door-bell ring she took her papers off the table. It would not have done to let " the boys" know she had been trying to write poetry. They would have made her life a burden to her.

SHE LAUGHED A GREAT DEAL AS SHE
WAS DOING IT.

But "Mamma" was different. Mamma always liked to be told about things, and perhaps the verses would make her laugh too. It was always nice to make her laugh.

So she took the exercise-book under her arm, and went upstairs with it, still flushed and elated by the excitement of composition.

Mamma was standing before the dressing-table taking off her nice little black bonnet. She never wore anything but black after " Poor Papa " died, though he died young.

She turned, smiling, as the Small Person approached with the exercise-book under her arm.

" Well, my dear? " she said. " What have you got there ? "

" I've got a piece of poetry," said the Small Person. " I want to read it to you and see if you don't think it's funny."

She forgot to say anything about having written it herself. She was so full of it and so eager to try it on Mamma that it seemed unnecessary to say it was her own. Just warm from the writing of it, she took it for granted that it was all understood.

She looked so elated and laughing that Mamma laughed too.

" What is it ? " she asked.

" Let me read it to you," said the Small Person. And she began. " It's called ' Alone,' " she said.

She began with the melancholy verse and did her best by it. Mamma looked a little mystified at first, but when the second verse began she smiled ; at the third she laughed her pretty laugh ; at the fourth she exclaimed " How funny ! " at the fifth and sixth she laughed more and more, and by the time all the others were finished she was laughing quite uncontrollably. The Small Person was flushed with delight and was laughing too.

"Do you think it's funny?" she asked.

"Funny!" exclaimed Mamma. "Oh, it is *very* funny! Where did you find it? Did you copy it out of one of the periodicals?"

Then the Small Person realized that Mamma did not know who had done it, and she felt rather shy.

"Where *did* you get it?" repeated Mamma.

The Small Person suddenly realized that there was an unexpected awkwardness in the situation. It was as if she had to confess she had been secreting something.

She became quite red, and answered almost apologetically, looking rather sheepishly at Mamma,

"I—didn't get it from anywhere." She hesitated. "I thought you knew. I—I wrote it myself."

Mamma's face changed. She almost dropped her bonnet on the floor, she was so astonished.

"You!" she exclaimed, looking almost as if she was a little frightened at such an astounding development. "You wrote it, my dear? Are you in earnest? Why, it seems impossible."

"But I did, Mamma," said the Small Person, beaming with delight at success so unexpected and intoxicating. "I really did. My own self. I was sitting in the drawing-room by myself. And I wanted to do something because it was so lonely—and the wind made such a noise. And I began to write—and I made it mournful at first. And then I couldn't go on with it, so I thought I'd make it funny. See, here it

is in the exercise-book—with all the mistakes in it. You
know you always keep making mistakes when you write
poetry."

Dear Mamma had never written poetry. It was revealed

"IT—WHY, IT IS SO CLEVER!"

afterward that "Poor Papa" had done something of the sort
before he was married. But never Mamma. And the rest
of the children—Aunt Emma's children and Aunt Caroline's

and Uncle Charles's—had never shown any tendencies of the
kind. And the Square children never did it. I think she
was a little alarmed. She may privately have been struck
with a doubt as to its being quite healthy. I am afraid she
thought it was enormously clever—and, in those days, one
not infrequently heard darkling stories of children who were
so clever that "it flew to the brain," with fatal results. And
yet, whatever her startled thoughts were, she was undis-
guisedly filled with delight and almost incredulous admiration.
She glanced at the exercise-book and looked up from it quite
blushing herself with surprise and pleasure.

"Well, my dear," she said, "you *have* taken me by surprise, I must confess. I never thought of such a thing. It
—why, it is so *clever!*"

And she put her arms about the overwhelmed and ecstasized
Small Person and kissed her. And for some reason her eyes
looked quite oddly bright, and the Small Person, delighted
though she was, felt a queer little lump for a moment in her
throat.

This being, I suppose, because they were both feminine
things, and could not even be very much delighted without
being tempted to some quaint emotion.

CHAPTER XII.

"EDITH SOMERVILLE"—AND RAW TURNIPS.

FIND it rather interesting to recall that, having had the amusement of writing the poem and the rapturous excitement of finding it was a success with Mamma, the Small Person did not concern herself further about it. It is more than probable that it had a small career of its own among her friends and relatives ; but of that she seems to have heard nothing but that it was read to a mature gentleman who pronounced it " clever.'   She did not inquire into the details and was given none of them.   This was discreet enough on the part of the older people.   She was not a self-conscious, timid child, to whom constant praise was a necessity.   She was an extremely healthy and joyous Small Person, and took life with ease and good cheer.   She would have been disappointed if Mamma had thought her "piece of poetry" silly and had not laughed at all.   As she had laughed so much and had been so pleased she had had all the triumph her nature craved, and more might have been bad for her. To have been led to attach any importance to the little effusion or to regard it with respect would certainly have been harmful. It is quite possible that this was the decision of Mamma, who probably liked her entire unconsciousness.

It was possibly, however, a piece of good fortune for her that her first effort had not been a source of discouragement to her. If it had been, it is likely that she would have done nothing more, and so would not have spent her early years in unconscious training, which later enabled her to make an honest livelihood.

As it was, though she wrote no more poetry, she began to scribble on slates and in old account books thrilling scenes from the Dramas acted with the Doll. It was very exciting to write them down, and they looked very beautiful when written—particularly if the slate-pencil was sharp—but the difficulty was to get a whole scene on to a slate. They had a habit of not fitting, and then it was awkward. And it happened so frequently that just at the most exciting point one's pencil would reach the very last line that could be crowded in and strike against the frame in the middle of a scene—even in the middle of a sentence. And it destroyed the sentiment and the thrill so to break off in such a manner as this :—

" Sir Marmaduke turned proudly away. The haughty blood of the Maxweltons sprang to his cheek. Ethelberta's heart beat wildly. She held out her snowy arms. ' Oh, Marmaduke !' she cried. ' Oh, Marmaduke ! I *cannot* bear it,' and she burst——"

You cannot get in any more when you come to the wooden frame itself, and it was trying to everybody—Sir Marmaduke Maxwelton included—not to know that Ethelberta simply burst into tears.

And it spoiled it to sponge it all out and continue on a clean slate. One wanted to read it all together and get the whole effect at once. It was better in old butcher's books, because there was more room, though of course the cook never had "done with them" until there were only a few pages left, and even these were only given up because they were greasy. Sometimes one had to scribble between entries, and then it might happen that when Ethelberta, " appalled by the sight of a strong man weeping, bent over her lover, laying her white hand upon his broad shoulder, and said, ' Marmaduke, what has grieved you so ? Speak, dearest, speak!' Sir Marmaduke turned his anguished eyes upon her, and cried in heart-wrung tones :—' Ethelberta—my darling—oh, that it should be so Onions 1d. Shoulder of Mutton 10s."

And old copy-books were almost as bad, though one sometimes did get a few more blank leaves. But with her knowledge of the impassioned nature of the descendant of the Maxweltons and his way with Ethelberta when he was expressing his emotions freely, the Small Person could *not* feel that " Contentment is better than riches," " Honesty is the best policy," " A rolling stone gathers no moss," were sentiments likely to " burst forth from his o'ercharged bosom

as he gazed into her violet eyes and sighed in tender tones "
—which not infrequently happened to him. Yes, it was
extremely difficult to procure paper. When one's maturity
realizes how very much there is of it in the world, and how
much might be left blank with advantage, and how much
one is obliged by social rules to cover when one would so far
prefer to leave it untouched, it seems rather sad that an
eager Small Person could not have had enough when she so
needed it for serious purposes.

But she collected all she could and covered it with vivid
creations. It was necessary that she should take precautions about secreting it safely, however. " The boys," having
in some unexplained way discovered her tendencies, were
immensely exhilarated by the idea, and indulged in the most
brilliant witticisms at her expense.

" I say!" they would proclaim, " she's writing a three-
volume novel. The heroine has golden hair that trails on
the ground. Her name's Lady Adolphusina."

They were not ill-natured, but a girl who was " romantic "
must expect to be made fun of. They used to pretend to
have found pieces of her manuscript, and to quote extracts
from them when there were people to hear.

It was great fun for the boys, but the frogs—I should say
the Small Person—did not enjoy it. She was privately a
sensitive and intensely proud Small Person, and she hated
it, if the truth were told. She was childishly frank, but
desperately tenacious of certain reserves, of which the story-

writing was one. She liked it so much, but she was secretly afraid it *was* a ridiculous thing for a little girl to do. Of course a child could not really write stories, and perhaps it was rather silly and conceited to pretend, even for amusement, that she was doing it. But she never let any one see what she wrote. She would have perished rather. And it really hurt nobody, however silly it was.

She used to grow hot all over when the boys made fun of her. She grew hot even if no one heard them, and if they began before strangers she felt the scarlet rush not only to the roots of her hair, but all among them, and to the nape of her neck. She used to feel herself fly into a blazing rage, but the realization she began her first conscious experience with at two years old—the complete realization of the uselessness of attacking a Fixed Fact—used to make her keep still. The boys were a Fixed Fact. You cannot stop boys unless you Murder them; and though you may feel—for one wild, rushing moment—that they deserve it, you can't Murder your own brothers. If you call names and stamp your feet, they will tease you more; if you burst out crying, they will laugh and say that is always the way with girls, so upon the whole it seems better to try not to *look* in a rage and keep your fury inside the little bodice of your frock. She was too young to have reached the Higher Carelessness of Theosophy and avoid feeling the rage. She was a mild creature when left alone to the Doll and the Story, but she was capable of furies many sizes too large for her. Irritable

she never was ; murderous she had felt on more than one
occasion, when she was not suspected of it.   She was a great
deal too proud to " let people see."   So she always hid her
scraps of paper, and secreted herself when she was covering
them.

Mamma knew and never catechized her about them in the
least, which was very perfect in her.   She doubtless knew
that in a rudimentary form they contained the charms which
enriched the pages of the *Family Herald* and the *Young
Ladies' Halfpenny Journal,* but she was too kind to interfere
with them, as they did not seem to interfere with " Pinnock's
England," or inspire the child with self-conscious airs and
graces.

My memory of them is that they were extremely like the
inspirations of the *Young Ladies' Halfpenny.*   The heroines
had the catalogued list of charms, which was indispensable
in the *Journal* type of literature.   One went over them carefully and left nothing out.   One did not say in an indefinite,
slipshod manner that Cecile was a blonde.   One entered
into detail, and described what she " had " in the way of
graces.   " She had a mass of silken, golden locks which fell
far below her tiny waist in a shower of luxuriant ringlets.
She had a straight, delicate nose, large pellucid violet eyes,
slender arched eyebrows, lashes which swept her softly-
rounded, rose-tinted cheek, a mouth like Cupid's bow, a brow
of ivory on which azure veins meandered, pink ears like
ocean shells, a throat like alabaster, shoulders like marble, a

waist which one might span, soft, fair arms, snowy, tapering,
dimpled hands, and the tiniest feet in the world. She wore
a filmy white robe, confined at her slender waist by a girdle
of pearl and gold, and her luxuriant golden tresses were
wreathed with snowdrops."

Heroines were not things to be passed over as mere
trivialities or every-day affairs. Neither were heroes. Sir
Marmaduke Maxwelton covered nearly two whole slates
before he was done with, and then entire justice was not
done to the "patrician air which marked all of Maxwelton
blood."

But how entrancing it was to do it. The Small Person
particularly revelled in the hair, and eyes, and noses. Noses
had always struck her as being more or less unsatisfactory,
as a rule, but with a pencil in one's hand one can " chisel "
them, and "daintily model" them; they can be given a
" delicately patrician outline," a "proud aquiline curve," " a
coquettish tilt," and be made Greek or Roman with a touch ;
and as to hair, to be able to bestow "torrents" of it, or
" masses," or "coils," or "coronals," or "clouds," is an
actual relief to the feelings. Out of a butcher's or green-
grocer's book there is a limit to the size of eyes, but within
their classic pages absolutely none.

Edith Somerville's hair, I remember distinctly, was golden-
brown. The weight of the "long, thick, heavy curls which
fell almost to her knee" was never stated, but my impression—the cold, callous impression produced by a retentive

memory drawing from the shades of the past the picture its
volume made on the Small Person's mind—my impression
would be that no mortal frame could have borne it about.
Edith Somerville would have been dragged to earth by it.
Her eyes were " large, soft, violet eyes," and were shaded by
"fringes" almost as long and heavy as her hair. But
neither of these advantages restrained her from active
adventure and emotions sufficiently varied and deep to have
reduced her to Hair Restorer as a stern necessity.

She was not created in a copy-book or recorded on a slate.
She was Told.

She began in school on one of the " Embroidery " Afternoons. On two or three afternoons each week the feminine
portion of the school was allowed to do fancy-work—to
embroider, to crochet, to do tatting, or make slippers or
cushions, with pink lap-dogs, or blue tulips, or Moses in the
Bulrushes on them in wool-work and beads. They were
delightful afternoons, and the reins of discipline were relaxed.

Sometimes some one read aloud, and when this was not
being done low-voiced talk was permitted.

It was not an uncommon thing for children to say to each
other :

" Do you know any tales to tell ? "

The Small Person, on being asked this question, had told
something more than once. But being asked on this special
afternoon by the little girl sitting next to her, she did not
reply encouragingly.

"I can't think of anything to tell," she said.

"Oh, try," said her small neighbour, whose name was Kate. "Just try; you'll remember something."

"I don't think I can," said the Small Person. "The things I know best seem to have gone out of my head."

"Well, tell an old one, then," urged Kate. "Just anything will do. You know such a lot."

The Small Person was making wonderful open-work embroidery, composed of a pattern in holes which had to be stitched round with great care. She hesitated a moment, then took a fresh needleful of cotton from the twisted coil which was kept thrown round her neck, so that it was easy to pull a thread out of.

"I don't want to tell an old one," she said; "but I'll tell you what I'll do, I'll make one up out of my own head."

"Make one out of your own head!" said Kate, with excitement. "*Can* you?"

"Yes, I can," answered the Small Person, with some slight awkwardness. "Don't you tell any one—but I sometimes make them up for myself—just for fun, you know—and write them on slates, but you can't get them all in on a slate."

"You *write* them!" Kate exclaimed, in a breathless whisper, staring at her with doubting but respectful eyes.

"Yes," the Small Person whispered back. "It's very easy."

"Why——" gasped Kate. "Why—you're an Auth'ress—like Charles Dickens."

"No, I'm not," said the Small Person, a little crossly, because somehow she felt rather ridiculous and pretentious. "I'm not. Of course that's different. I just make them up. It isn't a bit hard."

"Do you make them up out of things you've read?" asked Kate.

"No, that wouldn't be any fun. I just think them."

Kate gazed at her, doubtful respect mingling itself with keen curiosity. She edged closer to her.

"Make up one now," she said, "and tell it to me. Nobody will hear if you speak low."

And so began the first chapter of "Edith Somerville." It may have been the Small Person's liberality in the matter of the golden-brown hair, her lavishness as to features and complexion, and the depth and size of the violet eyes which fascinated her hearer. Suffice it to say she was bound as by a spell. She edged closer and closer and hung upon the words of the story-teller breathlessly. She had an animated little face and it became more animated with every incident. Her crotchet-work was neglected and she made mistakes in it. If there was a moment's interruption, for any reason whatever, the instant the cause was removed she snuggled excitedly against the Small Person, saying:

"Oh, go on, go on! Tell some more, tell some more!"

The Small Person became excited herself. She was not

limited by a slate-frame and she had the stimulus of an enraptured audience. She told "Edith Somerville" all the afternoon, and when she left the school-room Kate followed her while she related it on the way home, and even stood and told some more at the front gate. It was not finished when they parted. It was not a story to be finished in an afternoon. It was to be continued on the next opportunity. It was continued at all sorts of times and in all sorts of places. Kate allowed no opportunity or the ghost of one to slip by.

"Just tell a little ' Edith Somerville ' while we're waiting," she would say, whether it was in the few minutes before Miss Hatleigh came in, or in a few minutes when she was called from the room by some unforeseen incident, or on the way downstairs, or in the cloak-room, or waiting for the door-bell to be answered when the Small Person went home to her dinner or tea. It was not only the Embroidery Afternoons that were utilized, any afternoon or morning, or any hour would do.

For a short time the narrative was an entire secret. The Small Person was as afraid of being heard as she was when she entertained herself with the Doll. When any one approached she dropped her voice very low or stopped speaking. "What makes you so funny?" Kate used to say. " I wouldn't care a bit. It's a beautiful tale." And somehow one of the other little girls found out that the beautiful tale was being told, and Kate was made a go-between in the matter of appeal.

"Lizzie wants to know if she may listen?" the Small
Person was asked, and after a little hesitation she gave con-
sent and Lizzie listened, and a little later one or two others
attached themselves to the party. There were occasions
when three or four little girls revelled in the woes and
raptures of Edith Somerville.

THE WOES AND RAPTURES OF EDITH SOMERVILLE.

The relation lasted for weeks. It began with the heroine's
infancy and included her boarding-school days and the
adventures of all her companions of both sexes. There was
a youthful female villain whose vices were stamped upon her
complexion. She had raven hair and an olive skin, and she

began her career of iniquity at twelve years old, when she told lies about the nice blonde girls at the boarding-school, and through heartless duplicity and fiendish machinations was the cause of Edith Somerville's being put to bed—for nothing. She was always found out in the most humiliating way and covered with ignominy and confusion, besides being put to bed herself and given pages and pages of extra lessons to learn. But this did not discourage her; she always began again. An ordinary boarding-school would have dismissed her and sent her home in charge of a policeman, but this school could not have gone on without her. Edith Somerville would have had no opportunity to shine at all, and her life would have become a flat, stale, and unprofitable affair. Nothing could damp the ardour of the little female villain with the large black eyes. When they had left school, and Cecil Castleton, who had purple eyes and soft black hair, loomed up at Somerville Hall, with a tall, slender, graceful figure and a slender, silken moustache, then the female villain began to look about her seriously to invent new plots in which she could be unmasked, to the joy of all the blonde people concerned. Cecil Castleton's complexion was not olive and his hair was not raven—it was only black, and soft and wavy, and his eyes were purple, which quite saved him from being a villain. You *could* not be a villain if you had purple eyes. The female villain was naturally deeply enamoured of him, and wished to separate him from Edith Somerville. But of course it was no use. She would do

things it would take days to tell about, and the narration of
which would cause the school-room audience to gasp and
turn quite pale, but Cecil Castleton always found her out
after Edith Somerville and himself had suffered agonies.
And it almost seemed as if he could scarcely have helped
it. One might have imagined that she was extremely
careful to commit no crime which could not be exposed.
She was always dropping things where people would find them
when she had been listening, and she sat up at nights to
keep a diary about the lies she told and those she intended
to tell, and even wrote letters to her aunt that she might
gloat in black and white over the miseries and estrange-
ments she was planning. Sometimes she even put these
letters into the wrong envelopes, particularly when she intended to accept an invitation to take tea with Edith
Somerville's bosom friend. This feebleness of mind may,
like her character, have been the result of her complexion,
but it gave thrill and excitement to the story.

And how the audience was enthralled! It would be a
pleasing triumph for a story-teller of mature years to see
such eyes, such lips, to hear such exclamations of
delight or horror as this inchoate Small Person was
inspired by.

Naturally, stories told in school and at odd times meet with
interruptions.

"Young ladies, you are talking!" Miss Hatleigh would
say sometimes, or one would reach the front gate, or some

one would intrude, and then everything stopped. When it began again it began with a formula.

" ——And so—Edith came floating lightly down the broad old oak stairway while Cecil Castleton stood waiting below."

It always began "And so." That seemed to join it on to what had gone before. Accordingly, if the Small Person paused for a moment, Kate, whose property she had become, and who exploited her, as it were, and always sat next to her, would make a little excited movement of impatience in her seat, and poke her in the side with her elbow.

"And so——" she would suggest. "And so—and so—— Oh, do go on!"

And the others would lean forward also, and repeat: "And so?—And so?" until she began again.

The history of Edith Somerville being completed she began another romance of equal power.

It was also of equal length, extending over weeks of relation, and at its completion she began another, and another, and another. There is no knowing how many she told, but however her audience varied Kate always sat next to her. There were never more than two or three other listeners. The Tale Listeners were a little exclusive and liked to keep together.

It was through a brilliant inspiration of Kate's that a banquet became part of the performance. The Small

Person was extremely fond of green apples—very green and sour ones, such as can be purchased at the apple-stands only sufficiently early in the year to be considered unfit for human food. A ripe and rosy apple offered no inducements, but a perfectly green one, each crisp bite of which was full of sharp juice, was a thing to revel in.

Knowing this taste, Kate had the adroit wit to arrive one afternoon with her small pocket bulging.

" I've got something ! " she whispered.

" What is it ? "

" Something to eat while you're telling 'Edith Somerville.' Green apples."

They were such a rapturous success and seemed so inspiring in their effect that they founded a custom. The Listeners got into the habit of bringing them by turns. Green gooseberries were also tried, and soon Kate had another inspiration.

" If I can get a little jug downstairs," she whispered one afternoon, " I am going to fill it with water and bring it up hidden in my frock. And we can hide it under the form and take drinks out of it when no one is looking."

This may not appear to be a wildly riotous proceeding, but as jugs of water were not admitted into the school-room, and if one wanted a drink one went decorously downstairs first, the idea of a private jug and concealed libations was a daring and intoxicating thing.

Only Kate would have thought of this. She was a little

girl with a tremendous flow of spirits and an enterprising mind. She was sometimes spoken of by the authorities, rather disapprovingly, as " a Romp."

The Romp managed the feat of bringing up the jug of water. It was quite thrilling to see her come in as if she had nothing whatever concealed behind the folds of her skirt. She walked carefully and showed signs of repressing giggles as she approached the Listeners.

" Have you got it ? " whispered the Small Person.

" Yes—under my frock. I'll put it under the form."

It was put under the form, and, as soon as it was considered discreet, drinks were taken—sips out of the side of the jug, combined with green apples. Nobody was particularly thirsty, and if they had been there was plenty of water downstairs, but that was not contraband, it was not mingled with acid apples and " Edith Somerville."

There was a suggestion of delightful riot and dissipation in it. It was a sort of school-room Bacchanalian orgie, and it added to the adventures of Edith Somerville just the touch of license needed. The Small Person's enjoyment was a luxurious thing. To fill one's mouth with green apple and wash it down furtively from the jug under the form was bordering on perilous adventure. She was very fond of bordering on adventure. When apples were no longer green somebody brought raw turnips. Perhaps it was Kate again. She was a child with resources. Some of the girls seemed to like them. The Small Person did not, but she liked the sense of luxury and peril they represented. She was so pleased with the flavour of the situation that she bore up against the flavour of the raw turnips. She never told her fellow-banqueters that she did not enjoy them, that she found them tough and queer, and that it needed a great deal of water to wash them down. She took large bites and obstinately refused to admit to herself that they were on the whole rather nasty. To admit this would have been to have lost an atmosphere—an illusion. And she was very fond of her illusions. She loved them. She went on telling the stories and the Listeners hung on her words and nourished themselves with deadly indigestibles. And nobody died—either of " Edith Somerville " or the raw turnips.

CHAPTER XIII.

CHRISTOPHER COLUMBUS.

SHE told many stories "Continued in our Next," through many weeks, to the Listeners whose property she seemed to become. They had their established places near her. Kate's was the nearest, and, in fact, she was chief proprietress of the entertainment. She had been, as it were, the cause of Edith Somerville, who but for her never would have existed. My impression is that she arranged where the Listeners should sit, and that her influence was employed by outsiders who wanted to gain admission. She was an impetuous child, and did not like to lose time. If by some chance a Listener dropped out of the ranks for an afternoon, and, returning, asked anxiously :

" What did you tell yesterday? I didn't hear that part, you know ; " Kate would turn and give a hasty and somewhat impatient *résumé* of the chief events related.

" Oh, Malcolm came," she would say, " and Violet had a white dress with bluebells at her belt, and he was jealous of Godfrey, and he got in a temper at Violet, and they quarrelled, and he went away forever, and she went in a boat on the lake, and a storm came up, and he hadn't quite gone away, and he was wandering round the lake, and he plunged in and saved her, and her golden hair was all wet and tangled with bluebells, and so—" turning to the Small Person—" and so now go on!"

And then would proceed the recital describing the anguish and remorse of the late infuriate Malcolm as he knelt upon the grass by the side of the drenched white frock and golden hair and bluebells, embracing the small, limp, white hand, and imploring the violet eyes to open and gaze upon him once more.

They always did open. Penitent lovers were always forgiven, rash ones were reconciled, wickedness was always punished, offended relatives always relented—particularly rich uncles and fathers—opportune fortunes were left invariably at opportune moments. No Listener was ever harrowed too long or allowed to rust her crochet needles *entirely* with tears. As the Small Person was powerful, so she was merciful. As she was lavish with the golden hair, so she was generous with the rest. A tendency towards reckless liberality and soft relenting marked her for its prey even at this early hour. I have never been quite able to decide whether she was a very weak or a very determined creature—weak, because she could not endure to see Covent Garden merely as the costermongers saw it—or determined, because she had the courage to persist in ignoring the flavour of the raw turnip and bestowing on it a flavour of her own. After all, it is possible that to do this requires decision and fixedness of purpose. In life itself, agreeable situations are so often flavoured by the raw turnip, and to close one's eyes steadily to the fact that it is not a sun-warmed peach, not infrequently calls upon one's steadiness and resource.

If she had been a sharp, executive, business-like sort of child, she might have used her juvenile power as a thing with a certain market value. She might have dictated terms, made conditions, and gained divers school-room advantages. But she had no capacities of the sort. She simply told the stories and the others listened. If there had been a Listener astute enough in a mercantile way to originate the plan of privately farming her out, it might easily have been managed without her knowledge. She had been a stupidly unsuspecting little person from her infancy, and she might always have been relied upon for the stories. But there was no Listener with these tendencies, that I am aware of.

There came a time when some windfall gave into her possession an exercise-book which was almost entirely unused. She wrote her first complete story in it. It had been her habit previously to merely write scenes from stories on the slate and in the butcher's books. Sir Marmaduke Maxwelton and his companions were never completed. But the one in the blank-book came to a conclusion. Its title was "Frank Ellsworth, or Bachelors' Buttons." There was nothing whatever in it which had any connection with buttons, but the hero was a bachelor. He was twenty-two, and had raven hair, and, rendered firm by the passage of years of vast experience, had decided that nothing earthly would induce him to unite himself in matrimony. The story opened with his repeating this to his housekeeper, who was the typical adoring family servant. The venerable lady naturally smiled and shook her head with playful sadness—and then the discriminating reader knew that in the next page would loom up the Edith Somerville of the occasion, whose large and lustrous azure eyes and veil of pale golden ringlets would shake even the resolution of his stern manhood, and that, after pages of abject weakness, he would fall at her feet in a condition which could only be described as drivelling. My impression is that the story contained no evidence whatever of intelligence. But it was not at intelligence that the Small Person was aiming. She was only telling a story. She was very simple about it. She added the sub-title, "or Bachelors' Buttons," because she was pleased to see something in it vaguely figurative, and she liked the sound.

This story she read to Mamma, who said it was "a very pretty tale," and seemed somehow a little amused. Perhaps, after all, Mamma was clever. She never discouraged or made the Small Person feel her efforts silly and pretentious, but her gentle praise gave no undue importance to them, and somehow seemed to make them quite natural and innocent child developments. They were not things to be vain about, only things to enjoy in one's own very young way.

The Small Person obtained other blank-books and began

other stories, but none were ever finished. It always happened that a new one insisted on being begun and pushed the first aside. A very long one—the pride of her heart—called "Céleste, or Fortune's Wheel," was the guiding star of her twelfth year, but it was not concluded, and was thrown into the fire with all the rest when she left her own land for a new one.

The unfinished stories rather troubled her. When the infant regret that she was not a suitable subject for Sunday-school Memoirs had melted into a vague young desire not to have many faults, she used to wonder if the fact that so many stories were begun and not finished, was a sign of an undesirable mental quality.

"I ought to *finish* them," she used to think, remorsefully. "I ought not to begin things I don't finish." And she reproached herself quite severely.

" Shall I go on like this, and *never* finish one?" she thought, and she was vaguely distressed by a shadowing feeling that it might be her *sort* to be always beginning, and never finishing.

Inspired by her example, several of the Listeners began to write stories in old blank-books.

They were all echoes of Edith Somerville, and when they were given to her to read, she sternly repressed in herself any occasional criticism which arose in her small mind. She was afraid that criticism on her part, even though only mental, was a sign of what was generally spoken of as "a

bad disposition." She was, in private, extremely desirous
not to have "a bad disposition."

"I am conceited," she said to herself. "That is the
reason I don't think their stories are as nice as mine. It
is vulgar and ridiculous to be conceited, besides being
bad."

There was one Listener who described her hero, at an
interesting juncture, as " holding out his tiny lily hand," and
something within her was vaguely revolted by a sense of the
grotesque, but she could not have been induced to comment
upon the circumstance.

It might, in these days, be interesting to examine these
manuscripts—if they still existed—with a view to discovering
if they contained any germ of a reason why one child should
have continued to write stories throughout life, while the rest
did not write again. The romances of the Small Person were
wildly romantic and preposterously sentimental, without a
doubt. That there was always before her mind's eye a
distinct and strongly coloured picture of her events, I
remember ; the Listeners laughed and occasionally cried, and
were always rapt in their attention ; but if regarded with the
impartial eye of cold criticism, my impression is that they
might be dismissed as arrant nonsense. The story ran riot
through their pages, unbitted and unbridled.

But no one ever saw them but herself. Even Mamma
heard only the reading of "Frank Ellsworth." The rest,
scribbled in copy-books and blank-books, accumulated in

darkness and privacy, until the first great event of her life occurred.

It was a very great event, and, I am convinced, changed the whole colour of existence for her. It was no less a matter than leaving England, to begin a new life in America.

The events which preceded, and were the final reasons for it, were not pleasant ones. She was too young to be told all the details of them. But the beginning of it all was a sort of huge Story, which seized upon her imagination. It seemed to her that, for years and years, every one seemed to live, more or less, under the shadow of a cloud spoken of as " the War in America." This was probably felt more in the cotton manufacturing centres than anywhere else. Lancashire was the great county of cotton factories. Manchester was the very High Altar of the God Cotton. There were rich men in Manchester who were known everywhere as Cotton Lords. The smoke rolling from the tall Babel Towers which were the chimneys of their factories, made the sky dingy for scores of miles around, the back streets were inhabited by the men and women who worked at their looms, the swarms of smoke-begrimed children who played everywhere, began to work in the factories as early as the law allowed. All the human framework of the great dirty city was built about the cotton trade. All the working classes depended upon it for bread, all the middle classes for employment, all the rich for luxury. The very poor being wakened at four in the morning by the factory bells, flocked to the buildings over which the huge chimneys towered and rolled their volume of black smoke ; the respectable fathers of families spent their days in the counting-rooms or different departments of the big warehouses; the men of wealth lived their lives among cotton, buying and selling, speculating and gaining, or losing in Cotton, Cotton, Cotton.

" If the war in America does not end," it began to be said at one time, " there will be no more cotton, and the manufacturers will not know what to do."

But this was at first, when every one believed that the difficulty would settle itself in a few months, and the North and South would be united again. No one was pessimist enough to believe that such a terrible thing would happen as that the fighting would continue.

But after a while other things were said.

" There is beginning to be a scarcity of cotton. People even say that some of the factories may have to stop work."

Every closed factory meant hunger to scores of operatives —even hundreds. But still the war went on in America.

" Jackson's factory has stopped work because there is no cotton ! " came a little later.

Then :

" Bright's has stopped work ! All the operatives thrown out of employment. Jones is going to stop, and Perkins can only keep on about two weeks longer. They are among the biggest, and there will be hundreds on the street. Brownson's ruined. Had no cotton to fill his engagements.

All these enormously rich fellows will feel it awfully, but the ones who are only in moderate circumstances will go to smash ! "

It was oftenest the Boys who brought these reports. And still the war went on in America, and the Small Person heard rumours of battles, of victories and losses, of killed and wounded, of the besieging of cities with strange-sounding names, of the South overwhelmed by armies, of plantations pillaged, magnolia-embowered houses ransacked and burned. At least when she heard of Southern houses being destroyed, she herself at once supplied the magnolias. To her the South was the land of " Uncle Tom's Cabin." A plantation meant a boundless estate, swarming with negroes like Uncle Tom, Aunt Chloe, Eliza, and the rest of them, and governed either by a Legree or a St. Claire, who lived on a veranda covered with luxuriant vines and shaded by magnolia-groves, where Eva flitted about in a white frock and long, golden-brown ringlets.

She did not in the least know what the war was about, but she could not help sympathizing with the South because magnolias grew there, and people dressed in white sat on verandas covered with vines. Also, there were so many roses. How could one help loving a place where there were so many roses ? When she realized that the freedom from slavery of the Uncle Toms and Aunt Chloes and Elizas was involved, she felt the situation a strained one. It was impossible not to wish the poor slaves to be freed—the story

itself demanded it. One wept all through "Uncle Tom's
Cabin" because they had not their "freedom," and were
sold away from their wives and children, and beaten and
hunted with bloodhounds; but the swarms of them singing
and speaking negro dialect in the plantations were such a
picturesque and lovable feature of the Story; and it was
so unbearable to think of the plantations being destroyed,
the vine-covered verandas disappearing, and the magnolias
blooming no more to shade the beautiful planters in Panama
hats and snow-white linen. She was so attached to planters,
and believed them all—except the Legrees—to be graceful
and picturesque creatures.

But it seemed that the war prevented their sitting on their
verandas sipping iced juleps through straws, while their
plantations brought forth cotton.

Factory after factory closed, thousands of operatives were
out of work, there was a Cotton Famine. The rich people
were being ruined, the poor were starving, there was no
trade. The warehouses began to feel it, the large shops and
the small ones, more or less directly; all Manchester
prosperity depended upon Cotton, and as there was no Cotton
there was no money.

"If the war in America were only over," everybody said.

The stories of the starving operatives became as terrible
as the stories from America. Side by side with accounts of
battles there were, in the newspapers, accounts of the
"Lancashire Distress," as it was called. Funds were raised

by kind-hearted people in all sorts of places to give aid to the suffering creatures. There were Soup Kitchens established, and pitiful tales were told of the hundreds of hollow-eyed, ravenous men and women and children who crowded about their doors.

"If t' war i' 'Merica ud coom to an eend," they said among themselves, "we shouldna aw be clemmin."

And it was not only the operatives who suffered, all classes were involved as the months went on.

Little girls and boys began to say to each other:

"We can't go to Wales this summer. Papa says he can't afford it. There are so many of us and it takes such a lot of money. It's the war in America that makes him feel poor."

Or,

THE POOR WERE STARVING.

"The Blakes are not going to have a Christmas party. Mr. Blake has lost money through the war in America."

Or more awe-inspiring still:

"Do you know, Mr. Heywood is a bankrupt. The war in America has ruined his business, and he has to close his warehouse."

Even Mamma began to look harassed and anxious. She had neither a factory nor a warehouse, but she also had her difficulties and losses. Poor gentle and guileless little lady, she was all unfit to contend with a harsh, sharp, sordid world. She had tried to be business-like and practical, because poor Papa being gone, there were the three little girls to be taken care of and the boys to be given a career in life. Sometimes the Small Person found her at her dressing-table taking off her little black bonnet with gentle trembling hands and with tears in the blue eyes "Poor Papa" had thought like Amy Robsart's and Jeannie Deans's.

"Is anything the matter, Mamma?" she would ask

"Yes, dear," Mamma would answer, tremblingly. "I have a great deal to be anxious about. I am afraid I am not a very good business woman, and so many things go wrong. If I only had poor Papa to advise me——;" and the soft, deprecating voice would break.

"Don't, don't be low-spirited, Mamma," the Small Person would say, with a tremor in her own voice. "It will all come right after a while."

"Oh, my dear," Mamma would exclaim, at once tired and worn out, "nothing will *ever* come right until this dreadful war is over in America."

If this were a record of incidents, many might be recorded of this time. But it is only a record of the principal events which influenced the mental life of a Small Person.

There came at last a time when the war was ended, and

there was a pathetic story of the first bales of cotton being met by a crowd of hunger- and trouble-worn factory operatives with sobs and tears, and cries of rapturous welcome—and of one man—perhaps a father who had sat by a fireless hearth, broken of spirit and helpless, while his young swarm cried for bread—a poor gaunt fellow who, lifting his hat with tears running down his cheeks, raised his voice in the Doxology, one after another joining in, until the whole mass sang, in one great swelling chorus :

> " Praise God, from whom all blessings flow ;
> Praise Him, all creatures here below ;
> Praise Him above, ye Heavenly Host ;
> Praise Father, Son, and Holy Ghost."

The Small Person heard this story with a large lump in her throat. She felt that it meant so much, and that there must have been strange, sorrowful things going on in the cottages in the Back Streets.

It was after she had heard it that the great event occurred. She entered a room one morning to find Mamma and the two boys evidently discussing with unusual excitement a letter with a foreign post-mark.

" It seems so sudden ! " said Mamma, in rather an agitated voice.

" It would be a great lark," said one of the boys. " I should like it ! "

" I don't think I could ever make up my mind to leave

England!" fluttered Mamma. "It seems such a long way!"

The Small Person looked from one to the other.

"What is a long way?" she asked. "What are you talking about, Mamma?"

THE FIRST BALES OF COTTON.

Mamma looked at her, and her gentle face wore an almost frightened-like expression.

"America!" she said, "America!"

"America!" exclaimed the Small Person, with wide-opened eyes. "What about America?"

" We're going there," cried her younger brother, who was given to teasing her. " The whole job lot of us! I say, isn't it a lark ! "

" My dear, don't talk so thoughtlessly ! " said Mamma. " I have had a letter from your Uncle John, in America. He thinks it would be a good thing for us to go there. He believes he could find openings for the boys."

" Oh ! " gasped the Small Person. " America ! Do you —do you think you will go ? Oh, Mamma," with sudden rapture—" *do—do !* "

It seemed so incredibly delightful ! To go to America ! The land of Uncle Tom's Cabin ! Perhaps to see plantations and magnolias ! To be attended by Aunt Chloes and Topsys ! To make a long voyage—to cross a real Atlantic Ocean—in a ship which was not the Green Arm-Chair !

The real events of her life had been so simple and its boundaries had been so limited. From the Back Garden of Eden to the Square, and from the Square to the nearest mild sea-side town, which seemed to be made up of a Pier, bathing-machines, lodgings, and shrimps for tea, these were her wildest wanderings. The inhabitants of the Square were not given to travel. The Best Friend had spent a summer in Scotland, and the result of searching cross-examination as to her sojourn in this foreign land had seemed to give the whole flavour of Sir Walter Scott. She had sat by a " loch," and she had heard people speak Gaelic, which she had found an obstacle to fluent interchange of opinion. The Small Person had once seen a very little girl who was said to have come from America. She had longed to talk to her and find out what it was like to live in America—what America was like, what it was like to cross the Atlantic Ocean. Her craving was to find out all about America—to have it summed up as it were with definite

clearness. But the very little girl was only five years old, and she was not an intelligent little girl, and did not seem to regard herself as a foreign product, or to know that America was foreign and so intensely interesting. But the Small Person looked upon her with deference and yearning, and watched her from afar, being rather surprised that she did not seem to know how almost weirdly fascinating she was.

THE SMALL PERSON LOOKED UPON HER WITH DEFERENCE AND YEARNING.

And now to think that there was a possibility—even a remote one—that she might go to America herself!

"Oh, Mamma, please do, please *do!*" she said again and again, in the days that followed.

The Boys regarded the prospect with rapture. To them it meant wild adventure of every description. They were so exhilarated that they could talk of nothing else, and began to bear about them a slight suggestion of being of the world of the heroes of Captain Mayne Reid and Fenimore Cooper. They frequently referred to the "Deerslayer" and the "Last of the Mohicans," and brought in interesting details gathered from "a fellow I know, who comes from New York." Certain descriptions of a magnificent thoroughfare known as Broadway impressed the Small Person immensely. She thought that Broadway was at least half a mile wide, and that before the buildings adorning it Buckingham Palace and Windsor Castle must sink into utter insignificance—particularly a place called A. T. Stewart's. These opinions were founded upon the statements of the "fellow who came from New York."

It really was a delightfully exciting time. The half-awed rapture of hearing the possible prospect talked over by Mamma and the Uncles and Aunts, the revelation one felt one was making in saying to an ordinary boy or girl, "Do you know that *perhaps* we are going to America!" There was thrill enough for a lifetime in it.

And when at last Mamma "and the Aunts and Uncles and all the relations and friends" had decided the matter, and everybody went to bed knowing that they *were* going to

America, and that everything was to be sold and that the Atlantic *was* to be crossed, a new world seemed to be looming up, and the Small Person in the midst of her excitement had some rather queer little feelings and lay awake staring in the darkness and wondered who would get the Green Arm-Chair and the Nursery Sofa.

"GOOD-BYE," HE SAID, "I HOPE YOU WILL LIKE AMFRICA."

And then came greater excitement still. There seemed such thousands of things to be done and such a sense of intoxicating novelty in the air. Everybody was so affectionate and kind, and staying with a family of cousins while the house was disposed of seemed the most delightful rollicking thing. Two families in one house filled it to overflowing and produced the most hilarious results. There was laughing nearly all night, and darting in and out on errands and visits all day, there was a buying of things, and disposing of things, the seeing friends, the bidding good-bye, and somehow through it all that delicious sense of adventure and expectation and wild, young, good spirits and fun.

And this all reached a climax in an excited, entrancing journey to Liverpool, with two railroad carriages full of cousins, with an aunt or so in attendance. Then there was a night in Liverpool, in which it was almost impossible to sleep at all because there was so much to be talked over in bed, and the next morning was so thrillingly near and at the same time so unbearably far away.

And when it came at last, there came with it the sending away to the ship of cases and trunks, the bundling into cabs of all the cousins, with final packages of oranges and lemons and all sorts of remedies and resources, the tremulously delightful crowding on the wharf, the sight of the great ship, the nervous ecstasy of swarming upon it, exploring, exclaiming, discovering, glancing over the groups of fellow-passengers and singling out those who looked interesting. And then, while the excitement was at the highest, there came the ringing of the fateful bell, and the Small Person felt her heart give a curious wild thump and strange electric thrills run down into her fingers.

Suddenly she felt as if too much was happening all at once

—as if things were woful. She wanted to go to America—
yes, but everybody seemed to have his eyes filled with tears,
people were clinging to each other's hands,
shaking hands fiercely, clasped in each
other's arms, the people in the groups
about her were all agitated, Mamma was
being embraced by the aunts, with tears,
the cousins made farewell clutches, their
eyes suddenly full of tears.

"Good-bye, good-bye!" every one was
saying "Good-bye. I hope you'll be happy!
Oh! it's so strange to see you go! We
shall so miss you!"

The Small Person kissed and was kissed
with desperate farewell fer-
vour. People had not then
begun to make summer
voyages from America to
England every year. Going
to America was going to
another world — a world
which seemed divided from
quiet simple English homes
almost by the gulf of Eter-
nity.

"OH, DEAR! NOW I'M GOING TO AMERICA."

"Oh! good-bye, good-bye," she cried, quite passionately.
"I wish you were *all* going with us!"

A friend of an older cousin was of the party. He was a nice fellow she had known from childhood. Because he was nice enough to be trusted, she had given him her little dog, not knowing she might have taken it with her.

He was the last to shake hands with her. He looked rather nervous and deeply moved.

"Good-bye," he said, "I hope you will like America."

"Good-bye," she said, looking at him through tears. "You—I know you'll be good to Flora."

"Yes," he answered, "I'll be good to Flora."

And after looking at her a second he seemed to decide that she was still sufficiently a little girl to be kissed, and he kissed her wet cheek affectionately and walked away with an evident effort to maintain a decided air. And when the ship began to move slowly away, he stood with the aunts and cousins on the wharf, and they all waved their handkerchiefs, and the Small Person leaned upon the deck-rail, with tears running down her cheeks, and said to herself, under her breath :

"Oh, dear ! oh, dear ! *Now* I'm going to America."

CHAPTER XIV.

THE DRYAD DAYS.

THERE were many of them so beautiful—so newly, strangely beautiful—that words seem poor things to try and describe them with. Words are always poor things. One only uses them because one has nothing else. There is a wide, wide distance—a distance which is more than a matter of mere space—between a great murky, slaving, manufacturing town in England, and mountains and forests in Tennessee—forests which seem endlessly deep, mountains covered with their depths of greenness, their pines and laurels, swaying and blooming, vines of wild grape and scarlet trumpet-flower swaying and blooming among them, tangled with the branches of sumach and sassafras, and all things with branches held out to be climbed over and clung to and draped.

To have lived under the shadow of the factory chimneys, to have looked up at the great, soft, white clouds and fleecy, floating islands, always seeing them somewhat tarnished, as it were, with the yellowness of the chimney-smoke, to have picked one's daisies and buttercups in the public park, *always* slightly soiled with the tiny dots of black—the soft drift of "smuts" which never ceased falling—all this is an excellent preparation for rapture, when one is brought face to face with Dryad haunts, and may live Dryad days.

After the passing of the years in the Back Garden of Eden the Small Person had always been so accustomed to the ever-falling little rain of "smuts" that it had become an accepted feature of existence. They fell upon one's features, and one of the gentle offices of courtesy was to remove them from beloved and intimate cheeks or noses, and delicately direct the attention of mere acquaintances to their presence and exact situation. They made spots upon one's hat-ribbons, and disfigured one's best frock, and it occurred to no one to touch anything or rest against it without previous examination. In fact, one was so accustomed to their presence that the thought of resenting it rarely intruded itself, and one scarcely realized that there existed people who were not so rained upon. The Small Person had always felt it sad, however, that the snow—even the pure, untrodden, early morning snow—was spoiled so soon by the finer snow of black which fell upon its fair surface and speckled it. One of the most exciting nursery experiments in winter had been to put a cupful of milk, sweetened with nursery brown sugar, on to the window-sill outside, with the thrilling expectation that it would freeze and become ice-cream. This was always tried when it snowed—and one could get the milk and sugar;

but as Manchester weather was rarely very cold, the mixture
never froze, and if it had done so, it would never have become
ice-cream, or anything more nearly resembling it than pale-
blue skimmed milk and brown sugar would make. There had
been rare occasions when a thin coating of ice had formed
upon the top of the preparation, and been devoured with joy
—but it usually remained in a painfully sloppy condition,
and was covered with a powder of fine soot. And when in
despair one took it in and disposed of it with a spoon, with
an effort to regard it as a luxury, because *if* it had frozen it
would have been ice-cream—the flavour of smoke in it was
always its strongest feature. This was an actual trial to the
Small Person, because it interfered with the pretence that
it was ice-cream. It really was so horribly smoky. Everything had been more or less smoky all through her childhood.
And she had an absolute passion for the country. She
adored the stories in which people had parks or gardens, or
lived in rustic cottages, or walked in forests, or across moors,
or climbed "blue hills." She revelled in the thoughts of
bluebells and honeysuckles, and harebells and wild roses.
She "pretended" them in the Square itself. And this, by
the way, recalls a thrilling incident which is perhaps sufficiently illustrative to be worth recording.

One or two of the large vacant houses—perhaps all of
them—had once had large gardens behind them. Years of
neglect and factory chimney smoke had transformed them
into cindery deserts, where weeds grew rank in patches where

anything could grow at all, and where, despite the high brick walls surrounding them, all sorts of rubbish accumulated, and made both weeds and bareness more hideous, and their desolateness more complete. Usually the doors of entrance were kept locked, and there was no opportunity of even looking in from the outside. This fact the Small Person had always found enchanting, because it suggested mystery. So long as one could not cross the threshold, one could imagine all sorts of beautifulness hidden by the walls too high to be looked over, the little green door which was never unclosed. It made her wish so that she could get inside.

For years she never did so, but at last there came a rumour that the big houses were to be pulled down, to make room for smaller ones, and then it was whispered about among the Square children that the little green door in the high wall which surrounded the garden behind the big house, called for some mysterious reason "Page's Hall," had been opened, and some bold spirit had walked in and even walked out again.

And so there arrived an eventful hour when the Small Person herself went in—passed through the enchanted door and stood within the mysterious precincts looking around her.

If she had seen it as it really was she would probably have turned and fled. But she did not—she saw nothing as it was —*Grâce au Bon Dieu!* She saw a Garden. At least it had been a Garden *once*—and there were the high brick walls around it—and the little door so long unopened, and *once* there had been flowers and trees in it; they had really bloomed and been green and shady there, though it was so long ago. The charming treasure of her life had been the story that once the Square itself had been an ornamental lake with swans and lilies in it.

So she wandered about in a dream—" pretending." That changed it all. The heaps of earth and rubbish were mounds of flowers, the rough, coarse docks were lilies with broad leaves, every poor green thing struggling for life in the hard earth had a lovely name. They were green things at least, and she loved them for that. They *grew*—just as real flowers might have done—in a place which had once been a Garden.

All her little life she had felt a sort of curious kinship with things which grew—the trodden grass in the public park, the soiled daisies and buttercups. She had lived among her bricks and mortar and smoke with the yearnings of a little Dryad underlying all her pleasures. In the Square real trees and flowers and thick green ferns and grass seemed joys so impossible.

She walked about slowly. " Pretending " with all her power. She bent down and looked the weeds in their faces and touched them tenderly. They were such poor things, but in some places they grew quite thickly together and covered the ugly barrenness of the earth with a coarse, simple greenery which represented vaguely to her mind

something which was quite beautiful. She felt grateful to
them.

"Suppose they were roses and pansies and lilies and
violets," she said to herself. "How beautiful it would be!"

And then her dear Angel—the beloved Story—laid its kind,
beautiful hand upon her, and as she stood among the docks
and thistles, if an older person could have looked on—under-
standing—surely he would have seen light and colour and
glow come into her child face.

"You *are* roses!" she said. "You *are* violets—and
lilies—and hyacinths and daffodils and snowdrops! You
are!"

She had reached a mound and was standing on it. Beside
it, and between herself and the garden wall, there was a
sort of broad deep ditch, which seemed to have no reason for
existence, and offered no explanation of itself. The mound
had probably been formed by the piling up of the earth and
rubbish dug out and thrown up. The green things grew
over the mound and were rank even in the ditch itself,
scrambling down its ugly sides and half filling it. She looked
into this ditch and was pleased with it.

"This is the castle Moat," she said. "It is a Moat—and
these are the castle gardens."

The Moat enraptured her. It made all things possible.
She rambled about building around it.

"There is a Bower here," she said, in the very low voice
she reserved for such occasions. "It is a Bower covered

with roses. There are a great many trees—great big trees
with thick trunks and broad, broad branches. There are
oaks and beeches and chestnut-trees, and they spread their
boughs across the avenues from side to side. There are
Avenues. They are arched over with green. There are
banks and banks of flowers—banks of primroses and banks
of violets." She was always lavish. "There are bluebells
—and thick green grass and emerald velvet moss, and ferns
and ferns. There are fountains and Grottoes—and everything is *carpeted* with flowers."

It was all as abundant as Edith Somerville's hair.

And the Garden—the long dead Garden—the poor old,
forgotten, deserted Garden! Did it know that suddenly it
had bloomed again—as it had never bloomed before, even
half a century ago in its palmiest days?

It would be beautiful to believe that it did, and that some
strange, lovely struggle and thrill so moved it, that Nature
herself helped it to one last effort to live—expressing itself in
a mysterious and wonderful thing. If this was not so, how
did a flower grow there?

It seemed wonderful to the Small Person—though it was
such a tiny thing—such a common thing in some places that
there are country-bred people who would not have stooped to
pick it up. But she had never seen one.

She was bending over the green things on the mound and
telling them again that they were flowers—when she saw a
tiny red speck close to the ground.

It was scarcely more than a speck—and a flower was such a wildly improbable thing that she could not believe her eyes. "It's a *flower!*" she gasped. "A tiny red thing!" and

"I'VE FOUND A PIMPERNEL."

she knelt among the weeds and gloated on it. "It's a real flower!" she said, "*growing!*"

She did not know what it was. She took it up as if it had
been a holy thing. Only a little Dryad, who had spent her
life in the Square looking out at the slates for rain, could
have felt as she did. She looked at it closer and closer, and
then remembered something she had read in some poem of
rural scenes, the name of some little thing which was tiny
and red, and grew low and close to the earth. It did not
really matter whether she was quite right or not—she could
not know—but she loved the name and hoped it was the
real one.

"It is a Pimpernel," she said, "a scarlet Pimpernel. It
must be!" And she ended with a wild little shout to the
other children who were exploring within hail.

"Come here!" she cried. "Come here, and see what I
have found. I have found a Pimpernel—a scarlet Pimpernel
like those that grow in the fields!"

*   *   *   *   *   *

And from a life where a growing green thing was a marvel
and a mystery, and a pimpernel an incongruous impossibility,
she went into the Dryad days. They began with a journey
of two weeks after land was reached, with the banks of the
St. Lawrence, with days of travel through Canadian forests,
with speechless, rapt wanderings on the borders of a lake
like a sea, with short rests at cities which seemed new and
foreign, though they were populated with people who spoke
English, and which ended at last in a curious little village—
one unpaved street of wooden houses, some painted white

and some made of logs, but with trees everywhere, and forests and hills shutting it in from the world.

Then she *lived* in the Story. Quiet English people, who, driven by changes of fortune, wandered thousands of miles and lived without servants in a log-cabin, were a Story themselves. The part of the house which was built of logs enchanted her. It was quite like Fenimore Cooper, but that there were no Indians. She yearned inexpressibly for the Indians. There must have been Indians some time, and there must be some left in the forests. This was what she hoped and tried to find out about. It is possible her inquiries into the subject sometimes rather mystified the owners of the white wooden houses, to whom Indians seemed less thrilling. Occasionally an Indian or two were seen she found, but they were neither bloodthirsty nor majestic. They did not build wigwams in the forests, or wear moccasins and wampum ; they did not say " The words of the Pale Face make warm the heart of the White Eagle."

"They gener'ly come a-beggin' somepn good to eat," one of the white house-owners said to her. " Vittles, or a chaw er terbacker or a dram er whiskey is what *they're* arter. An' he'll lie *an'* steal, a Injun will, as long as he's a Injun. I hain't no use for a Injun."

This was not like Fenimore Cooper, but she persuaded herself that the people she questioned had not chanced to meet the right kind of Aborigine. She preferred Fenimore Cooper's, even when he wore his war-paint and was scalping the Pale Face—or rather pursuing him with that intent without attaining his object. She delighted in conversation with the natives—the real native, who had a wonderful dialect. As she had learned to speak Lancashire she learned to speak East Tennessean and North Carolinian and the negro dialect. Finding that her English accent was considered queer, she endeavoured to correct it and to speak American. She found American interesting, and rather liked it. That was part of the Story too. To use, herself, in casual conversation, the expressions she had heard in American stories related with delight in England was a joy. She used to wonder what the aunts and cousins and the people in the Square would think if they heard her say "I guess," and "I reckon," if they would be shocked, or if they would think it amusing.

The Square—the wet, shiny slates—the soiled clouds and falling soot seemed more than thousands of miles away—it was as if they could scarcely have been real, as if she must have dreamed them. Because she was really a Dryad she felt no strangeness in the great change in her life. It seemed as if she must always have lived with the vast clear space of blue above her, with hundreds of miles of forests surrounding her, with hills on every side, with that view of a certain far-off purple mountain behind which the sun set after it had painted such splendours in the sky. To get up at sunrise and go out into the exquisite freshness and scent of earth and leaves, to wander through the green aisles of tall, broad-

leaved, dew-wet Indian corn, whose field sloped upward behind
the house to the chestnut-tree which stood just outside the
rail-fence one climbed over on to the side of the hill, to climb
the hill and wander into the woods where one gathered
things, and sniffed the air like some little wild animal, to
inhale the odour of warm pines and cedars and fresh damp
mould, and pungent aromatic things in the tall " Sage
grass," to stand breathing it all in, one's whole being en-
veloped in the perfume and warm fresh fragrance of it, one's
face uplifted to the deep, pure blue and the tops of the pines
swaying a little before it—to hear little sounds breaking the
stillness when one felt it most—lovely little sounds of birds
conversing with each other, asking questions and answering
them and sometimes being sweetly petulant, of sudden brief
little chatters of squirrels, of lovely languorous cawing of
crows high above the tree tops, of the warm-sounding boom
and drone of a bee near the ground—strange as it may seem,
to do, to feel, to see and hear all this was somehow not new
to her. She was not a stranger here—she had been a stranger
in the Square when she had lifted her face to the low-
hanging, smoky clouds, talking to them, imploring them
when they would make no response. Without knowing why
—because she was too young to comprehend—she felt that
she had begun to be alive, and that before, somehow, she had
not been exactly living. Though the poor green things in a
smoke and soot-smitten Sahara had moved her and seemed
to say something vaguely, though one pimpernel astray

through some miracle among the rubbish had made her heart cry aloud, the full bounty of all Nature poured out before her in one magnificent gift seemed to be something she had always known—something she must have been waiting for all through her young years of exile—a native land which she could not have been kept away from always. And the most perfectly rapturous of her moments always brought to her a feeling that somehow—in some subtle way she was part of it—part of the trees, of the warm winds and scents and sounds and grasses. This—though she had not reached the point of knowing it—was because ages before— dim, far-off beautiful ages before, she had been a little Faun or Dryad—or perhaps a swaying thing of boughs and leaves herself, but this had been when there had been fair pagan gods and goddesses who found the fair earth beautiful enough for deity itself. And some strange force had reincarnated her in the Square.

It is worth mention, perhaps, that here she ceased to " pretend " in the old way. There was no need to " pretend." There were real things enough. She had laid the Doll aside reluctantly some time before—doing it gradually—after some effort at being purely maternal with it, which, after some tentative experiment, was a failure, because she so loved the real, warm babies that to hover over a wax one seemed an insult to her being. She lived in the woods, and she wrote stories on slates and pieces of paper. But the Story took a new tone. Sir Marmaduke Maxwelton was less prominent, and the hair of Edith Somerville flowed less freely over the pages. Hair and eyes seemed less satisfying and less necessary. She began to deal with emotions. She found emotions interesting—and forests and Autumn leaves assisted them and seemed part of them somehow, as she was part of the forests themselves. In the Square she had imagined—in the forests she began to feel.

She lived in the village long enough to gain a great deal of atmosphere, and then she went with the family to another place. The new home was not very far away from the first one, and though it was within a few miles of a place large enough to be called a town, instead of a village, it was even more sylvan. This time the house was a little white one and she did not deplore its not being built of logs, because she had lived beyond the Fenimore Cooper standpoint and expected neither Indians nor bears. She no longer regarded America as foreign, and had attained a point of view quite different from that of her early years.

The house was not at the foot of a hill, in these days it was at the top of one. It was not a very high hill, and the house was a tiny one, balanced quaintly on the summit, as if some flood had left it there on receding.

" Noah's Ark was left like it on Mount Ararat," said the Small Person. " Let us call it Noah's Ark, Mount Ararat. Think how queer it will look on letters." So it was called Noah's Ark, Mount Ararat, and the address *did* look queer on letters.

The house was a bandbox, but the place was adorable in these days. One stood on the little porch of Noah's Ark and looked out over undergrowth and woods and slopes and hills which ended in three ranges of mountains one behind the other. The farthest was the Alleghanies. It was at this place that what were most truly the Dryad days were lived. There were no neighbours but the woods, there was no village, the town was too far away to be visited often by people who must walk. There was nothing to distract one.

And the mountains always seemed to stand silently on guard. They became part of one's life. When the Small Person came out upon the porch very early in the morning they were deep purple and stood out soft and clear. The sun was rising from behind a hill to the left, where three or four very tall pine-trees seemed to have grown with a view to adding to the spectacular effect by outlining their feathery branches and straight, slender stems against the pink, pearl, amber, blue, apple-green, daffodil sky, growing intenser every moment until the golden flood leaped up above the tallest feathered pine. In the middle of the day they paled into faint blue in a haze of sunny light and heat, at sunset they were violet with touches of deep rose. The Small Person began to think of them as of human things. They were great human things, with moods which changed and expressions which came and went. She found herself going to look at them at all sorts of times, at different phases of the day or sky, to see how they looked now! They had

so many expressions—they always seemed to be saying something—no, *thinking* something—but she did not know what.
She would have been glad to understand—but with these too
she had that instinct of kinship—of somehow being part of
their purple, their clear dark outline, their dips and curves
against the sky—with these too! The first morning that she
went out and found them covered with snow—like ranges of
piled white clouds lightly touched with sunrise pink—she
almost cried out aloud!

But it was not only the mountains—all the near things
that surrounded and shut her in were of the same world.
She began to ramble and explore, wandering about, and led
on step by step by the things she saw until it ended in her
literally living in the open air.

About a hundred yards from the house was a little thicket
which was the beginning of the woods. Sassafras, sumach,
dogwood, and young pines and cedars grew in the midst of a
thick undergrowth of blackberry-vines and bushes. The
slender but full-branched trees stood very close together,
and a wild grape-vine roofed them with a tangled abun-
dance.

When she found this place the Small Person hungered to
get into the very heart of it and feel the leaves enclose her
and the vine sway about her and catch with tendrils at her
hair. But that was impossible then, because the briars and
undergrowth were so thick as to be impenetrable. For some
time it was a longing unattained.

It was a chance, perhaps, which caused it to be fulfilled. Some friend of the brothers, during a visit of some holiday, was inspired to suggest that an hour or so of vigorous cutting and pruning would do wonders for this very spot, and in a valiant moment the idea was carried out.

The Small Person lived in it for two years after, and it was called the "Bower."

The walls of the Bower were branches and bushes and lovely brambles, the ceiling was boughs bearing bravely the weight of the matted vine, the carpet of it was grass and pine-needles, and moss. One made one's way to it through a narrow path cleared between blackberry and wild-rose briars, one entered as if through a gateway between two slender sentinel sassafras-trees—and the air one breathed inside smelled of things subtly intoxicating—of warm pine and cedar and grape-vine blossoms made hot by the sun.

The Small Person was never quite sober when she lay full length on the grass and pine-needles on a Summer day and closed her eyes, dilating her little nostrils to inhale and sniff slowly the breathing of these strange sweet things. She was not aware that she was intoxicated, she only thought she was exquisitely happy and uplifted by a strange, still joy—better than anything else in life—something thrillingly near being the Party.

She came to the place so much, and spent so many hours there, lying on the grass, scribbling a bit of a story, sewing

a bit of a seam, reading, when she could get a book--which
was rarely—thinking out great problems with her eyes open
or shut, and she was so quiet that the little living things
actually became accustomed to her, and quite unafraid. It
became one of her pleasures to lie or sit and watch a bird
light upon a low branch quite near her, and sway there,
twittering a little to himself and giving an occasional touch
to his feathers, as he
made remarks about
the place. She would
not have stirred for
worlds for fear of
startling him. She
used to try
to imagine
what he
was say-
ing:

"Dear
me! what
a charm-

IT BECAME ONE OF HER PLEASURES TO WATCH A BIRD LIGHT UPON A
LOW BRANCH.

ing place! So delightfully fresh and cool after one has been
flying about in the hot sun. And so secluded! Why did
not Rosiebeak think of suggesting that I should build the
nest here? And none of those big, walking-about creatures
who don't sing——"

And then, perhaps, his round, bright, dark eye fell upon

her and made a nervous little move, as if he were going
to fly away, but seeing that she did not stir, reflected upon
her, and then she thought he said :

" What is it ? It looks like one of them, but it does not
move or make a noise, and its eyes look friendly."

And then he would gather courage, if he was an enterprising bird, and hop on to a nearer twig and examine
her, making quick little curious movements with his
head and neck. After which he would probably fly
away.

But she had an idea that he always came again and
brought some member of his family and endeavoured to
explain her to them and tell them that his impression was
that she would not hurt. Many of them, she was quite sure,
came again. She believed she recognized them. And they
became so used to seeing her that they did not mind her in
the least, and had quarrels and reconciliations, and said unpleasant things about their relations, and deplored the habits
their children were getting into, and practised their scales
just as if she had been one of the family.

Squirrels had no objection to her, rabbits occasionally
came and looked, and dragon-flies and beetles regarded her
as of no consequence at all.

" They think I am another kind of little animal," she used
to delight herself with thinking—" another kind of squirrel
or thrush or beetle, or a new kind of rabbit they have not
seen. Or perhaps they think I am a very little cow without

horns. They don't think I am a person, and they know I like them."

Some mornings she spent there it would be almost impossible to describe. The air, the odours, the sounds of insects and birds, the golden-green shade of the interlaced vines and branches, the delicate shadows of the leaves, the faint rustle of them, which only seemed to make the still-ness more still and full of meaning, wakened in her a fine, tender ecstasy, which did not seem to be exactly a feeling belonging to life on earth. She was always alone, and she used to lie in the gold-green shade quite motionless, with her eyes closed, a curious, rapt fancy in her mind.

"Somehow," she used to think, "I am not quite in my body. It is so beautiful that my soul is trying to get away like a bird. It has got out of my body and it is trying to break loose; but it is fastened with a little slender cord, and that holds it. It is fluttering and straining because it wants to fly."

There was even in her mind a perfectly definite idea of how high above her body the little soul hovered, straining to break the cord. She fancied it hovering, with the movement of a poised humming-bird, about a yard above her breast— no higher—the slender chain was only that long.

And she used to try to make herself more and more still, and centre all her thoughts upon the small lifted spirit— trying to help it to break the chain.

" If it could break it," she thought, "it would fly away—

I don't know where—and I should be dead. And they would come to the Bower to look for me at night when I did not come home, and find me lying here. And they would think it was dreadful and be so sorry for me; and nobody would know that I had only died because I was so happy that my soul broke the chain."

If in the young all things not quite of earth are justly to be considered morbid, then this ecstasy, too subtile to be called a mood, was a thing to be discouraged; but it was an emotion all of rapture, and was a thing so delicate and strange that she kept it silently to herself.

In the life she spent in wandering about the woods, she became perfectly familiar with all their resources. She was generally gathering flowers. The little house was filled with them to overflowing. Her hands were always filled as she rambled from one place to another. She was always looking for new ones, and it was not long before she knew exactly the spots of earth, of dryness or dampness, of shade or sun, in which each one grew. She was nearly always by herself, but she was never alone when she was among these intimates of hers. She found it quite natural to speak to them, to bend down and say caressing things to them, to stoop and kiss them, to praise them for their pretty ways of looking up at her as into the eyes of a friend and beloved. There were certain little blue violets who always seemed to lift up their small faces childishly, as if they were saying:

"Kiss me! Don't go by like that. Kiss me." That was what she imagined about them.

Those were lovely days when she found these violets. They were almost the very first things that came in the Spring. First there was a good deal of rain, and when one was getting very tired of it there would come a lull. Perhaps it was only a lull, and the sun only came out and went in with capricious uncertainty. But when the lull came the Small Person issued forth. Everything was wet and smelled deliciously—the mould, the grass, the ferns, and trees and bushes. She was not afraid of the dampness. She was a strong little thing, and wore cotton frocks. Generally she had no hat. A hat seemed unnecessary and rather in the way. She simply roamed about as a little sheep or cow would have roamed about, going where an odour or a colour led her. She went through the bushes and undergrowth, and as she made her way they shook rain-drops on her. As she had not known flowers before, and did not know people then, she did not learn the real names of the flowers she gathered. But she knew their faces and places and ways as she knew her family. The very first small flower of all was a delicate, bounteous thing, which grew in masses and looked like a pale forget-me-not on a fragile stem. She loved it because it was so ready and so free of itself, and it meant that soon the wet grass would be blue with the violets which she loved beyond all else of the Spring or Summer. She always lost her head a little when she saw the first of these small things, but when after a few days more rain, the sun decided to shine with warm softness, and things were pushing up through the mould and bursting from the branches and trunks of trees, and bluebirds began to sing, and all at once the blue violets seemed to *rush* out of the earth and purple places everywhere, she became a little mad—with a madness which was divine. She forgot she was a Small Person with a body, and scrambled about the woods, forgetting everything else also. She knew nothing but the violets, the buds of things, the leaves, the damp, sweet, fresh smell. She knelt down recklessly on the wet grass ; if rain began to fall she was not driven indoors unless it fell in torrents. To make one's way through a wood on a hillside with hands full of cool, wet leaves and flowers, and to feel soft, light, fresh rain-drops on one's cheek is a joy—a joy !

With the violets came the blossoming of the dogwood trees and the wild plum—things to be broken off in branches and carried away over one's shoulder, like sumptuous fair banners of white bloom. And then the peach- and apple-blossom, and new flowers at one's feet on every side as one walked through paths or made new ones through the woods. As the weather became warmer the colours became warmer with it. Then the early mornings were spent in the flower hunt, the heat of the day in the Bower, the evenings in the woods again, the nights upon the porch, looked down upon by myriads of jewels trembling in the vastness of dark blue, or by a moon, never the same or in the same setting, and always sailing like a boat of pearl in a marvellous, mysterious sea.

The Small Person used to sit upon the steps of the porch, her elbows on her knees, her hands supporting her chin, her face upturned, staring, staring, in the moments of silence. Something of the feeling she had had when she lay upon her back on the grass in the Back Garden of Eden always came back to her when she began to look up at the sky. Though it was so high—so high, so unattainable, yet this too was a world. Was she part of it too, as she was part of the growing things and the world they belonged to? She was not sure of that, but there was a link somewhere—she was something to it all—somehow! In some unknown way she counted as *something* among the myriads in the dark, vast blueness—perhaps for as much as a point of the tiniest star. She knew she could not understand, that she was beyond the things understandable, when she had this weird, updrawn, overwhelming feeling, and sat with her chin upon her hands and stared—and stared—and stared so fixedly and with such intensity, that the earth seemed gone—left far behind.

There was not a season of the year, an hour of the day which was not a wonderful and beautiful thing. In the winter there was the snow, the clear, sharp air, which seemed actually to sparkle, the rose and violet shadows on the mountains, the strange, lurid sunsets, with crimsons and scarlets and pale yellows, burning the summits of purple banks of cloud; there was the crisp sound of one's feet

treading the hardened snow, the green of the pines looking
emerald against the whiteness, the bare tree-tops grey or
black against the sky, and making the blue intenser; there
were the little brown rabbits appearing with cautious hops,
and poised, sniffing with tremulous noses, their large eyes
and alert ears alarming them at a breath of sound to a wild
skurry and disappearance into space itself. The rabbits were
a delightful feature. The Small Person never was able to
become intimate with them to the extent of being upon
speaking terms. They would come to the Bower and peep
at her in the Summer, but in the Winter they always disappeared with that lightning rapidity when they heard her.
And yet if they had known her she was conscious that they
would have recognized their mistake. She had always
deplored seeing them suspended by their hind legs in the
poulterers' shops in Manchester. They looked so soft, and
their dulled eyes seemed so piteous.

The Spring was the creation of the world—the mysterious,
radiant, young beginning of living. There were the violets
and dogwood blossoms, and every day new life. In the
summer there was the Bower, and the roses, and the bees,
and the warm, aromatic smells in the air. In the Autumn a
new thing came, and she seemed to have drunk something
heady again.

The first Autumn in America was a wondrous thing to her.
She existed from day to day in a sort of breathless state of
incredulity. In Manchester, the leaves on the trees in the

public park, being rained upon until they became sodden and brown, dropped off dispirited, and life was at an end. Even poetry and imaginative prose only spoke of "Autumn's russet brown."

But here marvels happened. After a few hot days and cool nights, the greenery of the Bower began to look strangely golden. As she lay under her prettiest sassafras-tree, the Small Person found, when she looked up, that something was happening to its leaves. They were still fresh, and waved and rustled, but they were turning pale yellow. Some of them had veins and flushes of rose on them. She gathered some and looked at them closely. They were like the petals of flowers. A few more hot days and cool nights and there were other colours. The maple was growing yellow and red, the dogwood was crimson, the sumach was like blood, the chestnut was pale gold, and so was the poplar—the trailing brambles were painted as if with a brush. The Small Person could not believe her eyes, as she saw what, each day, went on around her. It seemed like a brilliant dream, or some exaggeration of her senses.

"It can't really be as scarlet as that when one holds it in one's hand," she used to say at sight of some high-hued, flauntingly lovely spray.

And she would stand upon her tiptoes, and stretch and struggle to reach it, and stand panting and flushed, but triumphant, with it in her hand, finding it as brilliant as it had seemed.

She began to gather leaves as she had gathered flowers, and went about with bowers of branches, flaming and crimson, in her arms. She made wreaths of sumach and maple leaves, and wore them on her head, and put bunches in her little belt, and roamed about all day in this splendour, feeling flaunting and inclined to sing. Again, she did not know that she was not sober, and that, as Bacchantes of old wore wreaths of vine-leaves and reeled a little with the blood of the new grapes, so she was reeling a little with an exultation beautiful and strange.

There was a certain hollow in a little woodland road she loitered about a great deal, where there was a view which had always a deep effect upon her.

It was not an imposing view, it was a soft and dreamy one. The little road ran between woods and pretty wild places, to a higher land clothed with forest. The lovely rolling wave of it seemed to shut in the world she looked at when she stood in the little dip of the road, with wood on both sides and the mountains behind her.

When all the land was aflame with Autumn, and she sat on Indian Summer afternoons upon a certain large lichen-covered log, she used to gaze, dreaming, at the massed tree plumes of scarlet and crimson and gold uplifted against the blue sky, and softened with a faint, ethereal haze, until she had strange unearthly fancies of this too.

"A place might open in the blue," she used to say softly to herself. "It might open at any moment—now—while I am sitting here. And They might come floating over the trees. They would float, and look like faint, white mist at first. And if the place in the blue were left open, I might *see !*"

And at such times all was so *still*—so still and wonderful, that she used to find herself sitting breathless, waiting.

There were many memories of this hollow woodland path. So many flowers grew there, and there were always doves making soft murmurs and most tender, lovelorn plaints, high in the pines' far tops. She used to stand and listen to their cooing, loving it, and in her young, she-dove's heart plaining with them, she did not know or ask why.

And there, more than one rainy autumn day, she came and stood with her boughs in her arms, watching the misty rain veiling the sumptuous colours of the wooded hill, feeling, with a kind of joyful pleasure, the light-falling drops caressing her from her red-leaf wreaths to her damp feet, which mattered absolutely nothing. How could the wet grass she seemed to have sprung from earth with, the fresh cool rain she loved, hurt her, a young, young Dryad, in these her Dryad days ?

How many times it befell her to follow this road—sometimes running fast, sometimes stealing softly, sometimes breaking away from it to plunge into the wood and run again until she stopped to listen, looking up into some tree, or peering into a thicket or bush.

This was when she was giving herself up to what she called " the bird chases." She liked them so—the birds. She knew nothing of them. Birds such as the woods hold had not lived in the Square. There had been only serious-minded little sparrows nesting in the chimneys and in the gutterings. They brought up large families under the shadows of water-piping, and taught them to fly on the wet slates. They were grateful for crumbs, particularly in snowy weather, and the Nursery patronized them. But they were not bluebirds with a brief little trill of Spring carolled persistently from all sorts of boughs and fence corners; they were not scarlet birds with black velvet marks and crests; they were not yellow birds like stray canaries, or chattering jays, or mocking-birds with the songs of all the woods in their throats; they were not thrushes and wrens, or woodpeckers drumming and tapping in that curiously human way.

As there had been no one to tell her the actual names of the flowers, so there was no one to tell her the real names of the birds. She used to ask the negroes who lived at the foot of Mount Ararat, but the result was so unsatisfactory that she gave it up.

"What is that little bird that sings like this, Aunt Cynthy?" she would say, trying to imitate its note. "It is a little blue thing."

"That's the bluebird," seemed rather incomplete to her at the outset.

"And the bright red one with the black marks and crest?"

"That's the redbird," which did not seem much more definite.

"I can *see* they are blue and red," she used to say. "Haven't they a name?"

But they had no other name, and when the birds described were less marked in colour there seemed to be no names at all. So she began to commit the birds to memory, learning their notes and colours and forms by heart. In this way were instituted the bird chases.

If she heard a new song or note she ran after it until she saw the bird and could watch him piping or singing. It was very interesting and led her many a mile.

Sometimes she believed birds came and sang near her, under cover, for the mere fun of leading her through the woods. They would begin on a tree near by and then fly away and seem to hide again until she followed them. She always followed until she caught sight of her bird. But they had wonderful ways of eluding her, and led her over hill and dale, and through thicket and brambles, and even then sometimes got away.

There was one with a yellow breast and a queer little cry which she pursued for several days, but she saw him at last and afterward became quite familiar with him. And there was one, who was always one of two—a tender, sad little thing who could never be alone, and who was always an unanswered problem to her, and somehow, above all, her best beloved. It was a mystery because no one ever seemed to have seen it but herself, and her description of it was never recognized.

It was a little bird—a tiny one, a soft, small, rounded one, with a black velvet cap, and on its first appearance it came and sat upon the rail of the veranda, and waited there, uttering a piteous little note. She knew that it was waiting and was calling to its mate because it was a timid little thing, existing only under the cover of his wing and love. He could only be a small creature himself, but the Small Person felt that in the round, bright, timid eyes he was a refuge from the whole large world, the brief, soft, plaintive cry for him was so pathetically trustful in its appealing.

The Small Person, who was sitting on the wooden steps, was afraid to stir for fear of frightening her.

"You poor little mite," she murmured, "don't be so sorrowful. He'll come directly."

And when he did come and was lovingly rejoiced over, and the tiny pair flew away together, she was quite relieved.

There was something in the brief, plaintive note which always led her to follow it when she heard it afterward, which only happened at rare intervals. There seemed to be some sad little question or story in it which she could not help wishing she could understand. But she never did, though each time she heard the sound she ran to look for it, and stood beneath its tree looking up with a sense of a persistent question in her own breast. What was it about? What did it want? What was it sad for? She never heard the tiny thing without finding it huddled down patiently upon some bough or spray, calling for its mate. And to her

it never had any other name than the one she gave it of
" The little mournful bird."

These Dryad days were of the first years of her teens.
They were the early Spring of her young life. And she was
in Love—in Love with morning, noon, and night; with
Spring and Summer and Winter; with leaves and roots and
trees; with rain and dew and sun; with shadows and odours
and winds; with all the little living things; with the rapture
of being and unknowingness and mere Life—with the whole
World.

CHAPTER XV.

"MY OBJECT IS REMUNERATION."

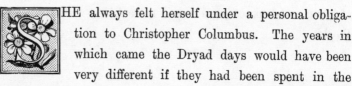HE always felt herself under a personal obliga-
tion to Christopher Columbus. The years in
which came the Dryad days would have been
very different if they had been spent in the
Square or within reach of it. Reduced resources in a
great town or city where one has lived always, mean change
of habits and surroundings, shabbiness, anxiety, and annoyance. They mean depression and dreariness, loss of courage,
and petty humiliations without end. In a foreign land
among mountains and forests they mean seclusion, freedom,
and novelty. It is novelty to live in a tiny white house, to
wait upon one's self and every one else, to wear a cotton frock
and chase birds through the woods without the encumbrances
of hats and gloves and parasols. It is also freedom. But in
Dryad days lived in an unsylvan age a serious reduction of
resources is felt. Detail seems unnecessary, but, without
entering into detail, it may be stated that this reduction of
resource was felt on the summit of Mount Ararat. Alas! one
cannot live always in the Bower, one must come home to

dinner and to bed. Material and painful but unavoidable. Even cotton frocks wear out and must be washed. And the openings for the Boys had not been of sufficient size to allow of their passing through to ease and fortune. The consequences were curious sometimes and rather trying.

"We are decayed ladies and gentlemen," the Small Person used to say to herself. "We ought to be living in a ruined feudal castle and have ancient servitors who refuse to leave us and will not take any wages. But it is not at all like that." It was not at all.

It was so very unlike it that there were occasions when she gathered her leaves and flowers with a thoughtful little frown on her forehead, and when she talked the matter over with Edith or Mamma. Edith was the practical member of the family.

"If one could *do* something!" she said, thoughtfully.

But there are so few things to do if one is very young and quite inexperienced and lives on the top of Mount Ararat.

Still the serious necessity increased and she pondered over it more and more.

"I wish I *could* do something," she said next. She began to have long discussions with Edith as to what one might invent as a means of resource—what one could teach or learn—or make. But nothing proved practicable.

There was a queer little room with unfinished wall and rafters where she had a table by a window and wrote stories in wet or cold weather when the Bower was out of the question. There was no fireplace and she used to sit wrapped in a shawl for warmth. She had a little cat which always followed her and jumped upon the table when she sat down, curling up in the curve of her left arm. The little cat's name was Dora, and it was also a Small Person. It had a clearly defined character, and understood that it was assisting in literary efforts. It also added to the warmth the shawl gave. Edith used to come upstairs to the rough little room and talk to her, and gradually she got into the habit of reading to her pieces of the stories. She began with extracts —speeches, scenes, chapters—and led on by the delight of her audience, which was stimulating as that of the Listeners, she read all she wrote.

Edith was a delightful listener. She was an emotional little being, and exquisitely ready with tears, and uncontrolled in laughter. She was at the same time a remarkable Small Person and singularly perceptive.

They used to sit and talk over the stories—telling each other what they liked best or were not quite sure of. The Small Person had a curious feeling that in reading to Edith she was submitting her creations to a sort of infallible critic —one who was infallible not through experience or training, but through a certain unfailing truth of sentiment and emotion, and an unfaltering good taste. It must be recorded, however, that neither of them for a moment contemplated the chance of a larger public existing for the stories. Never

for an instant had it occurred to the Small Person that they
were worth publishing. That would have seemed to her a
height of presumption quite grotesque. They were hidden
from the Boys as carefully as ever, and derided as mercilessly
when they were mentioned by them. "Frances's love

WITH THE LITTLE CAT CURLED UP IN HER LEFT ARM.

stories" were an unfailing source of jocular entertainment.
It was never ill-natured entertainment, and there was plenty
of rough young wit in it; but naturally a young Briton finds
it rather a lark to contemplate the thought of a small girl he

has chaffed and patronized all his life secreting herself to write pages of romantic description of the emotions of "a case of spoons." The Boys were fond of her, and their intercourse was marked by bounteous good-nature and the best of tempers and spirits, but their impression naturally was that the stories would be "bosh." But she continued to write them—with the little cat curled in her left arm—and read them to Edith. It was the "Answers to Correspondents" in various magazines which inspired her with her tremendously daring thought. Things like these:

"Elaine the Fair.—Your story has merit, but is not quite suited to our columns. *Never* write on both sides of your paper."

"Christabel.—We do not return rejected manuscript unless stamps are enclosed for postage."

"Blair of Athol.—We accept your poem, 'The Knight's Token.' Shall be glad to hear from you again."

She read them on the final pages of *Godey's Lady's Book* and *Peterson's Magazine*, etc. Her circumstances were not sufficiently princely to admit of her being among the subscribers, but occasionally a copy or so drifted in her way. They were much read at that time in the locality.

She was reading these absorbing replies to the correspondents one day when a thought floated into her mind, and after a few moments of indefiniteness took shape and presented itself before her. She blushed a little at first because it had such an air of boldness. She rather thrust it aside, but after a while she found herself contemplating it as if from afar off.

"I wonder how much they pay for the stories in magazines?" she said, reflectively, to Edith.

Edith did not know, naturally, and had not formed any opinion.

"I wonder if they pay much," the Small Person continued; "and—what sort of people write them?" It seemed impossible that ordinary every-day people could write things that would be considered worth paying for and publishing in magazines. It seemed to imply immense talents and cultivation and training and enormous dignity.

She did not think this because she found the stories invariably brilliant, but because she felt that there must be some merit she was not clever enough to detect; if not they would never have been published.

"Sometimes they are not so *awfully* clever," she said.

"Well," said Edith, boldly "I've seen lots of them not half as nice as yours."

"Ah!"—she exclaimed, conscious of being beset by her sheepish feeling—"that's because you are my sister."

"No, it isn't," said the valiant Edith, with her favourite little pucker of her forehead. "I don't care whether I'm your sister or not. Some of your stories are beautiful!"

The Small Person blushed, because she was of the Small Persons who are given to superfluous blushing. "I wonder," she said, "if the magazine people would think so."

"I don't think anything about magazine people," said Edith; "but I don't see why they shouldn't think so."

"They wouldn't," said the Small Person, with a sudden sense of discouragement. "Of course they wouldn't."

But she could not help the thought of the answered correspondents, returning to her afterward. She found herself wondering about them as she rambled through the woods or lay on the grass in the Bower. How did they send their stories to the magazines? Was it by post or by express? If it was by post how many stamps would it take? How could one find out? It would be important that one should put on enough. She remembered "answers" such as this. "March Hare.— We cannot receive MSS. on which insufficient postage has been paid." It was evidently necessary to make a point of the postage.

Then there was the paper. To meet the approval of an august being it seemed as if something special must be required. And more than once she had read instructions of such a nature as: "Airy, Fairy Lilian.—Write in a clear hand on ordinary foolscap paper."

She was only fifteen, and her life had been spent between the Square and the Bower. Her horizon had not been a broad one, and had not embraced practical things. She had had no personal acquaintance with Ordinary Foolscap. If the statement had demanded extraordinary foolscap she would have felt it only natural.

Somehow she found a timid, but growing interest in the whole subject. She could not quite get away from it. And when circumstances occurred which directed her attention specially to the results of the reduced resources she was led to dwell on it with a certain sense of fascination.

" Something *must* be done ! " she said to herself desperately. " We can't go on like this. Some one *must* do something."

The three little girls talked together at times quite gloomily. They all agreed that Somebody must do something. The Boys were doing their best, but luck did not seem to be with them.

" Something *must* be done," the Small Person kept repeating.

" Yes," replied Edith, " but what must it be and Who will do it ? "

The people whose stories were bought and printed must some time have sent their first stories. And they could not have known whether they were really good or not until they had asked and found out. The only way of finding out was to send one—written in a clear hand on *one* side of ordinary foolscap—having first made quite sure that it had stamps enough on it. If a person had the courage to do that, he or she would at least hear if it was worth reading—if a stamp was enclosed.

These were the reflections with which the Small Person's mind was occupied.

And if it was worth reading—if the August Being deigned

to think it so—and was not rendered rabid and infuriate by insufficient postage, or indistinct writing, or by having to read on both sides of the ordinary foolscap, if he was in need of stories for his magazine, and if he was in a good temper he might accept it—and buy it.

If the Listeners had liked her stories so much, if Edith and Edwina liked them, if Edith thought they were as nice as some she had read in *Godey's Lady's Book*, might it not be just possible that—that an Editor might deign to read one and perhaps even say that it "had merit," even if it was not good enough to buy. If he said that much, she could study the stories in the *Lady's Book*, etc., assiduously enough, per- haps, to learn the secret of their success, and finally do something which might be worthy to compete with them.

She was a perfectly unassuming child. She had never had any feeling about her story-telling but that it seemed part of herself—something she could not help doing. Secretly she had been afraid, as time went by, that she had been Romantic with the Doll, and in private she was afraid that she was Romantic about the stories. The idea that any one but the Listeners and Edith and Edwina would be likely to care to hear or read them had never entered her mind. The cheer- ful derision of the Boys added to her sensitive shyness about them, and upon the whole she regarded her little idiosyncrasy as a thing to be kept rather quiet. Nothing but actual stress of circumstances would have spurred her to the boldness of daring to hope for them. But in those days Noah's Ark found itself lacking such common things—things which could not be dispensed with even by the most decayed of ladies and gentlemen.

So one day after many mental struggles she found herself sitting alone with Edith and the little cat, in the small room with the bare walls and rafters. And she gathered her courage in both hands.

"Edith," she said, "I've been thinking about something."

Edith looked at her with interest. She was a lovely little person and a wonderful friend for her years—which were thirteen.

"What is it?" she said.

"Do you think—do you *think* it would be silly to send one of my stories—to a magazine—and see if they would take it."

I cannot help believing that at the first moment Edith rather lost her breath. The two were English children brought up in a simple English nursery in the most primitively conventional way. Such a life is not conducive to a spirit of boldness and enterprise. In matters of point of view they would have seemed to the American mind incredibly young for their years. If they had been American children they would have been immensely cooler and far less inclined to ultra-respectful attitudes toward authority.

"Do you?" said the Small Person. "Do you?"

Edith gathered herself together also. Across a lifetime the

picture of her small face rises with perfect distinctness. She was a fair little person, with much curling blonde hair and an expressive little forehead which had a habit of puckering itself. She was still startled, but she bore herself with a courage which was heroic.

"No," she answered, " I don't ! "

If she had said that she did, the matter might have ended there, but as it was, the Small Person breathed again. She felt the matter might be contemplated and approached more nearly. One might venture at least to talk about it in private.

"I have been thinking and thinking about it," she said. " Even if they are not good enough to be published it would not do any harm just to try. They can only be sent back— and then I should know. Do you think we dare do it ? "

" If I were you I would," said Edith.

" I believe," hesitated the Small Person, "I do believe I will."

Edith began to become excited.

" Oh," she said, " I think it would be splendid ! What would you send ? "

"I should have to write something new. I haven't any-thing ready that I should care to send. I'd write something carefully—just as well as I could. There's a story I began to write when we lived in the Square, three years ago. I never finished it, and I only wrote scenes out of it in old account-books ; but I remember what it was about, and the other day

I found an old book with some scraps of it in. And I really
do think it's rather nice. And I might finish it, perhaps.
She began to tell the story, and became exhilarated with the
telling, as she always did, and Edith thought it an enchanting story, and so it was decided that it should be finished and
put to the test.

" But there's one thing," she said, " I would not have the
Boys know for anything in the world. They would laugh so,
and they would think it such a joke if it was sent back again.
I'm going to put in stamps to send it back with, because if
you put on stamps enough they will send it back. And
perhaps they wouldn't take the trouble to write a letter if
they didn't like it, and I didn't send the extra stamps. You
often see in magazines a notice that manuscript will be
returned if stamps are sent. So in that way I shall be sure
to find out. But I must get them without the Boys knowing."

" Yes, you must," said Edith. "They *would* tease you so
if it came back. But what are you going to do ? You know
there isn't any money now but what the Boys get. And
that's little enough, goodness knows."

" We shall have to think about it," said the Small Person,
" and contrive. It will take a good deal of contriving, but I
have to write the story first."

" Do you think it will take many stamps ? " asked Edith,
beginning to pucker her expressive little forehead, anxiously.

" Yes, a good many, I'm afraid," was the Small Person's

answer. "And then we have to buy the foolscap paper—
ordinary foolscap. But of all things promise and swear you
won't breathe a word before the Boys."

It was a marvel that they did not betray themselves in
some way. It was so thrilling a secret. While the story
was being written they could think and talk of nothing else.
The Small Person used to come down from the raftered
Temple of the Muses with her little cat under her arm, and
her cheeks a blaze of scarlet. The more absorbed and interested she was the more brilliant her cheeks were.

"How red your cheeks are, my dear," Mamma would say.
"Does your head ache?"

But her head did not ache, though it would have done, if
she had not been a splendidly strong little animal.

"I always know when you've been writing very fast,"
Edith used to say; "your cheeks always look so flaming red."

It was not long, of course, before Mamma was taken into
confidence. What she thought it would be difficult to say,
but she was lovable and sustaining as usual.

"It won't do any harm to try, dear," she said. "It seems
to me you write very nice things, for any one so young, and
perhaps some of the editors might like them ; and, of course,
it would be a great help if they would pay you a little
money."

"But the Boys mustn't know one word," said the Small
Person. "I'll tell them if it's accepted, but if it isn't, I'd
rather be dead than that they should find out."

And so the story went on, and it was read aloud under the rafters, and Edith revelled in it, and the little cat lay curled up in the Small Person's left arm, quite undisturbed by the excitement in the atmosphere around her. And as the work went on the two plotters discussed and planned and contrived.

First, how to get the ordinary foolscap to copy out the manuscript in a beautiful clear hand; next, how to get the address of the Editor to be approached; next, how to address him; next, how to find out how many stamps would be necessary to carry the fateful package and bring it back, if such was to be its doom.

It had all to be done in such secrecy and with such precautions. To walk to town and back was a matter of two or three hours, and the Boys would wonder if they did not hear why a journey had been made. They always saw the person who went to town. Consequently no member of the household could go without attracting attention. So some outsider must be found who could make the journey to visit a bookstore and find the address required. It would have been all so simple if it had not been for the Boys.

But by the time the story was finished an acquaintance who lived on a neighbouring farm had procured the address and some information about the stamps, though this last could not be applied very definitely as the weight of the package could only be guessed at, in the absence of letter scales.

The practical views of the Small Person at this crisis impress me greatly. They were so incompatible with her usual vagueness and romancings that they strike me as rather deliciously incongruous.

"I must have the right kind of paper," she argued, "because if I sent something that seemed queer to them they would think me silly to begin with. And I must write it very plainly, so that it will be easy to read, and on only one side, because if they are bothered by anything it will make them feel cross and they will hate me, and hate my story too. Then, as to the letter I send with it, I must be very careful about that. Of course they have a great many such letters and they must be tired of reading them. So I must make it very short. I would send it without a letter, but I must make them understand that I want it sent back if they don't like it, and call their attention to the stamps and let them know I am doing it for money and not just for the fun of getting the story published."

"How will you tell them that?" asked Edith, a trifle alarmed. It seemed so appalling and indelicate to explain to an Editor that you wanted money.

The Small Person felt the same thing. She felt this sordid mention of an expectation of receiving dollars and cents in return for her work a rather gross thing—a bold thing which might cause the Editor to receive a severe shock and regard her with cold disgust as a brazen Small Person. Upon the whole, it was the most awful part of the situation. But there

was no help for it. Having put her hand to the plough she
could not turn back, or trifle with the chance that the Editor
might think her a well-to-do Small Person, who did not write
stories for publication through sheer need but for amusement.

"I shall have to think that over," she said, seriously. "I
don't want to offend them, of course, but I *must* tell them
that!"

If it were possible to depict in sufficiently strong colours
her mental impressions of the manners, idiosyncrasies, and
powers of an Editor, the picture would be an interesting one.
It was an impression so founded upon respect and unbounded
awe. Between an utterly insignificant little girl in the
mountains of East Tennessee, and an Editor in a princely
official apartment in Philadelphia or New York, invested by
Fate with the power to crush people to the earth and reduce
them to impalpable dust by refusing their manuscripts—or to
raise them to dizziest pinnacles of bliss by accepting them—
there was a gulf imagination could not cross. Buddha himself, sitting in rapt passiveness with folded hands and down-
dropped lids, was not so marvellous or so final. Editors presented themselves to her as representing a distinct super-
human race. It seemed impossible that they were moved by
the ordinary emotions and passions of mankind. Why she
was pervaded with a timorousness, with regard to them,
which only Mad Bulls or Tigers with hydrophobia would have
justified, it is not easy to explain. Somehow the picture of

an Editor rendered infuriate—"gone *must*," as it were—in consequence of an inadequacy of stamps, or a fault in punctuation, or as a result of indistinct handwriting covering *both* sides of the ordinary foolscap, was a thing which haunted both her waking and sleeping hours.   He would return the manuscript with withering comment, or perhaps not return it at all, and keep all the stamps, which might be considered perfectly proper for an Editor if one broke his Mede and Persian laws.   Such a being as this must be approached with salaams and genuflections, and forehead touching the dust.

Poor, little, anxious girl; I find her—rather touching at this distance—sitting in her raftered room, scribbling hotly, with her little cat in her arm, and her cheeks like scarlet flame.   But she could not write the explanatory letter to the Editor until she had got the money to buy the paper to copy the story and the stamps to send it.   And how to do this without applying to the Boys?   The rafters and the little cat presided over hours of planning and discussion.   What could be done?

"If we could make some money ourselves," said the Small Person, mournfully.

"But we can't," said Edith.   "We've tried, you know."

"Yes," said the Small Person.   "Embroidery — and people don't want it.   Music lessons—people think I'm too young.   Chickens—and they wouldn't hatch, and when they did they died of the gapes; besides the bother of having to

sit on the hen to make her sit on the nest, and *live* at full
speed round the yard chasing them back into the coops when
they get through holes. Out of all that setting of goose-
eggs only one hatched, and that wasn't a goose—it was a
gander—and a plank fell on it and killed it."

They both indulged in a rueful giggle. The poultry-raising
episode had been a very trying and exciting one.

" If we had something to sell," she went on.

" We haven't," said Edith.

The Story touched the Small Person sadly on the
shoulder.

"It would be awfully mournful," she said, "if I really
could write stories that people would like—and if I could sell
them and get money enough to make us quite comfortable—
if all that good fortune was in me—and I never found it out
all my life—just because I can't buy some paper and postage-
stamps."

It seemed too tragic. They sat and looked at each other
in gloom. The conversation ended after a short time in
desperate discouragement, and the Small Person was obliged
to wander out to her hollow on the woodland road, and stand
for a long time looking at the changing trees, listening with
a strange feeling to the sorrowful plaining of the doves on
the tops of the pine-trees.

As the leaves were changing then, it cannot have been very
long before the inspiration came which solved the problem.
Who gave the information which gave rise to it is not a detail

which any one can remember. Something or other makes it
seem probable that it was Edwina, who came into the writing
room one day, and sat down saying, *à propos* of nothing in
particular :

"Aunt Cynthy's two girls made a dollar yesterday by selling wild grapes in the market. They got them in the woods
over the hill."

"Which hill ? " asked the Small Person.

"The hill near the house—the one you can see out of the
window. They say there are plenty there."

"Are there ? " said the Small Person.

"I wonder how much they got a gallon ? " said Edith.

"I don't know," said Edwina. "But they sold a dollar's
worth, and they say they are going to gather more."

"Edith ! " exclaimed the Small Person, " Edith ! "

A brilliant idea had come to her. She felt her cheeks grow
hot.

"Suppose," she said, " suppose *we* went and gathered some
—a whole lot—and suppose we gave the girls part of the
money to sell them for us in the market—perhaps we should
get enough to buy the stamps and paper."

It seemed an inspiration of the gods. It was as if some
divine chance had been given to them. Edith and Edwina
clapped their hands. If wild grapes had been sold they
would sell again ; if the woods were full of them why should
they not gather them—quarts, gallons, bucketfuls of them—
as many as necessity required ?

There arose an excited, joyous gabbling at once. It would be delightful. It would be fun in itself. It would be like going gypsying. And if there were really a great many grapes, they might be sold for more money than would pay for the stamps.

"It's a good thing we are not living in the Square now," said the Small Person. "We couldn't go and gather wild grapes in Back Sydney Street."

Suddenly they felt rich and hopeful. *If* they found grapes enough—*if* they were sold—*if* the Editor was in a benign humour, who could tell what might happen.

"If they buy this one," said the Small Person, "I can write others, and perhaps they will buy those too. I can always make up stories. Wouldn't it be queer if it turned out *that* was the thing I have to do? You know how we have kept saying 'Something *must* be done.' Oh, Edith! wouldn't it be beautiful?"

"Of course it would be beautiful," answered Edith.

"Perhaps," sighed the Small Person, "it is too nice to be true. But we'll go and get the wild grapes."

And so they did.

It was Edith who arranged the detail. She saw the little mulatto girls and talked with them. They were greatly pleased at the idea of selling the grapes. They would pilot the party to places where they believed there were vines, and they would help in the gathering, themselves. The expedition began to wear the air of an exhilarating escapade.

It would have been a delightful thing to do, even if it had been arranged merely as a holiday. They issued forth to conquer in the wildest spirits. Each one carried a tin bucket, and each wore a cotton frock, and a sun-bonnet or a utili-

THEY CHASED ABOUT THE WARM YELLOWING WOODS LIKE WILD THINGS.

tarian straw-hat. The sun was rather hot, but the day was a golden one. There was gold in the trees, gold in the air, gold in the distances. The speculators had no decorum in their method. They chased about the warm yellowing woods like wild things. They laughed and shouted to each other when they scrambled apart. They forced their way through undergrowth, and tore their way through brambles; they clambered over great logs; they uttered wild little shrieks at false alarms of snakes; they shouted with joy when they came upon vines; they filled their buckets, and ate grapes to repletion, and swung on the rope-like vines themselves.

The Small Person had never been less sober. At intervals she roamed away a little, and stood in some warm, golden place, with young trees and bushes closed about her, simply breathing the air, and enraptured with a feeling of being like a well-sunned Indian peach. Her cheeks had such an Autumn heat in them—that glow which is not like the heat of Summer. And what a day of dreams! If—if—if! "If" is such a charming word—such a benign one—such a sumptuous one. One cannot always say with entire sense of conviction, "I have a kingdom and a princely fortune, and I will build a palace of gold,"—but who cannot say, "*If* I had a kingdom and the fortune of a prince, I would build a palace of gold?" The golden palace rises fair, and one almost hears the courtiers speak. "If" gives a shadow, the substance of which would be a poorer thing.

She built her palaces that day, and furnished them, and *lived* in them, as she searched for her wild grapes. They were innocent palaces, and small ones, for she was a very young and vague thing; but they were things of light, and love and beauty, and filled with the diaphanous forms of the beliefs and dreams only such young palaces can hold.

The party went home at sunset with its tin pails full to the brim and covered with fresh vine-leaves.

" We shall get two or three dollars for these," said one of the pilots. " Me an' Ser'phine didn't have nigh onto as many that other time."

" Now if they sell them," said Edith and the Small Person when they got home, " we shall have the paper and the postage-stamps."

It seems to be regretted that the amount they sold for can-not be recalled—but it was enough to buy the postage-stamps and paper and pay all expenses, and even leave something over. The business part of the speculation was a complete success.

With what care the ordinary foolscap was chosen; with what discreet precautions that it should be of the right size and shade, and should not enrage the Editor the instant he saw it. How large and round and clear each letter was made in the copying. An Editor who was afflicted with cataract might have read it half-way across his palatial sanctum. And then the letter that was written to accompany the venture! How it was reflected upon, and reasoned about, and discussed! " An Editor does not want to know anything about *me*," the Small Person said. " He does not know me, and he doesn't care about me, and he won't want to be bothered. I shall just say I have enclosed the stamps to

send the manuscript back with, if he does not want it. And
I shall have to speak about the money. You see, Edith, if
the stories are worth writing, they must be worth reading,
and if they are worth printing and reading they must be
worth paying for, and if they are not worth publishing and
reading they are not worth writing, and I had better not
waste my time on them." Whence this clear and practical
point of view it would be difficult to say. But she was quite
definite about it. The urgency of the situation had made
her definite. Perhaps at a crisis she became practical—but
it was only at a crisis.

And after serious deliberation and much rewriting and
elimination the following concise and unmistakable epistle
was enclosed in a roll of manuscript with enough extra
stamps to have remailed an Editor :

" Sir :

"I enclose stamps for the return of the accompanying MS., 'Miss Desborough's Difficulties,' if you do not find
it suitable for publication in your magazine. My object is
remuneration.

> " Yours Respectfully,
>
> " F. Hodgson."

This was all except the address, which was that of the
post-office of the neighbouring town. Both Edith and herself were extremely proud of the closing sentence. It
sounded so business-like. And no Editor could mistake it.

And if this one was offended it positively could not be helped."

" And it's true," she said.   " I never should have dreamed of sending a thing to an Editor if I hadn't been *obliged* to. My object *is* remuneration."

And then they could not help breaking into childish giggles at the comical aspect of their having done a thing so bold, and their ideas of what the Editor would think if he could see the two curly and innocent Small Persons who had written that unflinchingly mercenary sentence.

CHAPTER XVI.

AND SO SHE DID.

T is a simple enough matter to send a story with a serene mind to Editors one knows, and of whom one is aware that they possess the fine intellectual acumen which leads them to appreciate the boon bestowed upon them, and the firmness to contemplate with some composure the fact that one's " object is remuneration." But it is quite a different affair to send one's timid and defenceless first-born into the cave of an unknown dragon, whose fangs may be dripping with the blood of such innocents.

Oh, the counting of the hours which elapse before it reaches its destination, and the awful thrill of realizing that perhaps at the very hour one is living through, the Editor is Reading it ! The Small Person did not lose any quakings or heart-beats to which she was entitled by the situation. She experienced them all to the utmost, and even invented some new ones. She and Edith quaked together.

It was so awful not to know anything whatever, to be so

blankly ignorant of editorial habits and customs.   How long
did an Editor keep a manuscript before he accepted it, or put
all the stamps on with a blow and sent it back ?   Did he
send it back the day after he had read it, or did he keep it
for months or years ?   Might one become old and grey without
knowing whether one's story was accepted or rejected ?   If
he accepted it, would he send the money at once or would he
wait a long time, and how much would it be when it came ?
Five dollars—ten—twenty—a hundred ?   *Could* it possibly
be as much as a hundred !   And if it *could* be a hundred—
oh ! what things could be done with it, and how everybody
could live happily forever after !

"I could write one in a week," the Small Person said.
"That would be *four hundred* dollars a month !   Oh ! no,
Edith," breathlessly, "it *couldn't* be a hundred ! "   This was
because it seemed impossible that any one could make four
hundred dollars a month by her stories and really retain her
senses.

She felt it was better to restrain such frenzy and discipline herself by putting it as low as possible.

"Suppose it is only about a dollar," she said.   "I'm sure
it's worth more, but they might be very stingy.   And we
want money so much—we are so *obliged* to have it, that I
suppose I should be forced to let them have it for a dollar
and even go on writing more."

"It *couldn't* be as little as that," said Edith.

"It would be rather cheap even for me," said the Small

Person, and she began to laugh a little hysterically. "A dollar story!"

Then she began to make calculations. She was not at all good at calculations.

"The magazine costs two dollars a year," she pondered. "And if they have fifty thousand subscribers, that would make a hundred thousand dollars a year. They haven't *many* stories in each number. Some of the magazines have more than fifty thousand subscribers! Edith," with a little gasp, "suppose it was a thousand dollars!"

They vibrated like pendulums from light-headed ecstasy to despair.

"They'll send it back," she said, in hopeless downfall, "or they'll keep the stamps and they won't send it back at all, and I shall wait weeks, and weeks, and weeks, and never know *anything* about it. And all this thinking and hoping and contriving will have gone for worse than nothing!"

She ended with tears in her eyes, half-laughing at herself because they were there, and she was an emotional Small Person, who had also a sense of the humour of her own exaggerations. She was a creature who laughed a great deal, and was much given to making her sisters and brothers laugh. She liked to say ridiculous things and exaggerate her views of a situation until they became grotesque and she was obliged to laugh wildly at them herself. "The family's Ups and the family's Downs" were a source of unbridled jokes which still had a touch of usefulness in them.

" I laugh instead of crying," she used to say. " There *is* some fun in laughing and there isn't any in crying, and it *is* ridiculous in one way."

She made many of these rueful jokes in the days that followed. It seemed as if these were months of days and the tension became more than was bearable. It is likely that only a few weeks passed.

But at last—at last something came. Not the manuscript with all the stamps in a row, but a letter.

And she and Edith and Mamma and Edwina sat down panting to read it.

And when it was read they could not understand it!

The letter was not preserved, but the memory of the impression it created preserved itself.

Somehow it seemed strangely vague to their inexperienced minds. It began—thank God—by praising the story. It seemed to like it. It plainly did not despise it at all. Its sole criticisms were on the unceremonious abbreviation of a name, and an intimation that it was rather long. It did not say it was refused, but neither Edith nor the Small Person were at all sure that it meant that it was accepted, and it said nothing about the Remuneration.

" Have they accepted it ? " said the Small Person.

" They haven't rejected it," said Edith.

" They evidently think it is rather good," said Mamma.

" I don't know exactly what they mean," the Small

Person finally decided, but I believe it has something to do with the Remuneration."

Perhaps it had, and perhaps it had not. Perhaps greater experience might have been able to reach something technical in it they could not see. They read and re-read it, thought and reasoned, and invented translations. But the only conclusion they could reach was that perhaps Remuneration not being the Editor's object, was his objection, and that he thought that by adroit encouragement and discouragement he might obtain the prize without the Object.

So after a little waiting the Small Person wrote to ask for its return. In after years she was frequently puzzled by her memory of that first letter. She never knew what it had meant. Experience taught her that it was curiously unbusiness-like, and inclined her to believe that in some way it was meant to convey that the objection was the Remuneration.

Then the story was sent to another Editor.

"I'll try two or three times," the Author said to Edith. "I won't give up the first minute, but I won't keep on forever. If they don't want it, that must mean that it isn't good enough."

The story—whose real name was not "Miss Desborough's Difficulties," but something rather like it—was one she had planned and partially written in her thirteenth year, in the Square. One or two cherished scenes she had written in the old account-books. Many years later, on being exhumed from among old magazines in the Congressional Library, and read again, it revealed itself quite a respectable, but not in the least striking, story of love, estrangement, and reconcilia- tion between a stately marvel of English young-lady beauty and good-breeding, and the stalwart, brave, and masculine British officer, who was separated and suffered with her in high-bred dignity and fine endurance. It was an evident— though unconscious—echo of like stories in *Cornhill, Temple Bar*, and *London Society*. The Small Person had been much attached to these periodicals. Its meritorious features were a certain reality of feeling in the people who lived in it, and a certain nice quality in the feeling itself. However trifling and romantic the plot, the officer was a nice fellow and a gentleman, the beauteous English maiden had good manners, and her friends, the young married people, were sympathetic and sweet-tempered. It moved with some dramatic touch and had an air of conviction. Otherwise it had no particular qualities or originality.

Did months elapse again before they heard from the second Editor—or was it years? Perhaps it was only weeks, but they contained several protracted lifetimes.

And then! Another letter! Not the manuscript yet!

"Sir:

"(They were immensely edified at being called Sir.) Your story, 'Miss Desborough's Difficulties,' is so distinctly English that our reader is not sure of its having been written by an American. We see that the name given us for the address is not that of the writer. (The Samaritan friend had lent his name—that the mail might evade the Boys.) Will you kindly inform us if the story is original ?

"Yours truly," etc.

This was the letter in effect. It would be impossible to recall the exact words.

Shaken to the centre of her being the Small Person replied by the next mail.

"The story is original. I am English myself, and have only been a short time in America."

The Editor replied quite promptly :

"Before we decide will you send us another story ? "

How they were elated almost to delirium ! How delighted Mamma's smile was ! How the two unliterary ones exulted and danced about.

"It will be Accepted ! It will be Accepted ! It will be Accepted ! " they danced about exclaiming.

"Perhaps the Editor will buy them both ! " said Edith. "That will be *two* instead of one ! "

The Small Person went up to the raftered room positively trembling with joy and excitement. The Editor did not believe she had written her own story. He would not believe it until she wrote another. He would see ! She would show him ! "

The little cat lay curled up in her arm for three days, seeming lulled by the endless scratching of the pen. She said nothing, but perhaps in some occult feline way she was assisting. The Small Person's cheeks blazed hotter and hotter. She felt as if she were running a race for life or death. But she was not tired. She was strung up to the highest and intensest pitch. The Story was good to her. Her best beloved, who had stood by her all her vivid short life—making dull things bright and bright things brilliant— who had touched the face of all the world with a tender, shining hand—who had never deserted her—did not desert her now. Faithful and dear fair shadow of things, how passionately she loved it! In three days the new story was finished. It was shorter than "Miss Desborough," but she knew it was as good, and that the Editor would see it was written by the same hand. But she made it an American story without a touch of English colouring. And the grapes had brought enough money for more postage-stamps.

She did not walk for the next few days—she danced. She chased about the woods wildly, gathering more flowers and leaves and following more birds than ever. Sometimes when she went to the hollow in the road she felt as if she might be lifted from her feet by the strange exhilaration within her, and carried away over the variegated tree-tops into the blue.

Her stories were of some use after all. They were not altogether things to be laughed at because they were Romantic. Somehow she felt almost as if she were vindicating and exalting a friend who had been kind and tender, and yet despised. Ah, how *good* it was! *If* all would go well—if she might go on—if she need be ashamed no longer —but write openly as many stories as she liked—how *good* to be alive! She was so young and ardent, she knew nothing and believed *everything.* It might have been arranged by Fortune that she should get the fullest, finest flavour of it. When the answer came they were passing through one of "the Family's Downs." That was their manner of describing the periods when everything seemed at its worst; when even the Boys, who were robustly life-enjoying creatures, wished "something would turn up." Nothing is more trying than to feel that one's sole hope is that "something may turn up." The something usually turns down.

And on one of these days the Letter came. Standing by a table in the bare little room, the Small Person opened it with quivering hands, while Mamma and Edith looked tremblingly on.

She read it, rather weakly, aloud.

"Sir :

"We have decided to accept your two stories, and enclose payment. Fifteen dollars for 'Aces or Clubs,' and twenty dollars for 'Miss Desborough's Difficulties.' We shall be glad to hear from you again.

"Yours truly," etc.

She gave a little hysterical laugh, which was half a gasp.

"They—they've accepted it," she said, rather obviously to Edith, "and they've sent me thirty-five dollars.'

"THIRTY-FIVE DOLLARS!" HE EXCLAIMED, STARING AT HER.

"Well, my dear," said Mamma, quite tremulously, "they really were very nice tales. I could not help thinking so."

" They are Accepted," cried Edith, quite shrill with ecstasy. " And they will take more. And you can go on writing them all your life."

And just at that moment—as if it had been arranged like a scene in a play, one of the Boys came in. It was the elder one, and rather an intimate of the Small Person, of whom he was really quite fond, though he considered her Romantic, and having a strong sense of humour, his witticisms on the subject of the stories had been well worth hearing.

" What's up? " he said. " What is the matter with you all? "

" Come out on the Porch," said the Small Person.

Why she was suddenly overwhelmed with a sort of shyness, which embraced even Mamma and Edith, she could not have told.

" Well," he said, when they stood outside.

" I've just had a letter," said the Small Person, awkwardly. " It's—it's from an Editor."

" An Editor! " he repeated. " What does that mean? "

" I sent him one of my stories," she went on, feeling that she was getting red. " And he wouldn't believe I had written it, and he wrote and asked me to send another, I suppose to prove I could do it. And I wrote another—and sent it. And he has accepted them both, and sent me thirty-five dollars."

" Thirty-five dollars! " he exclaimed, staring at her.

" Yes," she answered. " Here's the cheque."

And she held it out to him.

He took it and looked at it, and broke into a good-natured, delighted, boyish laugh.

"Well, by Jove!" said he, looking at her, half-amused and half-amazed. "That's first-class, isn't it? By Jove!"

"Yes," she said, "it is. And they want some more. And I am going to write some—as many as I can—a whole lot!"

And so she did.

But she had crossed the delicate, impalpable dividing line. And after that, Life itself began, and memories of her lose the meaning which attaches itself to the memories of the Mind of a Child.

THE END.